ANCHORED

IN THE

WORD

ANCHORED

IN THE

WORD

*Daily Decrees and Declarations
for Faith, Spiritual Growth,
and Divine Alignment*

Franny Onokha Ofunne

DEDICATION

This book is dedicated to YOU.

To the believer who has carried silent battles, whispered prayers, and unwavering faith through seasons of waiting, stretching, and becoming. To every heart that has chosen faith in moments of uncertainty, and to every soul that has spoken God's Word while still waiting to see it fulfilled.

It is for those who have prayed through weariness, stood firm in the face of opposition, and continued to believe even when the journey felt long. For those learning to trust God again, one declaration at a time, releasing former things, standing daily on His Word, and choosing to speak life even when circumstances speak otherwise.

This book is also deeply dedicated to my husband, Daniel, and to my sons, David, Donald, and Damian. To my sisters, Vera, Pachaline, and Moyo, and to my brother, Pius, you are my covering, my encouragement, and my daily reminder of God's faithfulness. Thank you for your prayers, your patience, and for standing beside me through every season of growth. Your love, strength, and unwavering support have carried me more than you know. This journey has been steadied by your presence and strengthened by your faith.

Above all, this book is dedicated to God, whose Word is living, powerful, and unfailing, the One who heals, restores, defends, provides, and faithfully completes every work He begins.

May these pages remind you that God is near, His promises are sure, and His strength is active in every season of your life.

You are seen.
You are strengthened.
You are called.

And God is still doing a new thing in YOU!

PREFACE

WORSHIP is a sacred invitation into alignment with God's heart. Through praise, thanksgiving, and spoken truth, we are gently drawn into His presence and reminded of who He is and who we are in Him. We are called to lift our voices with joy, to serve the Lord with gladness, and to enter His presence with thanksgiving not only in moments of ease, but in every season of life. This posture of worship prepares the heart to receive truth, respond in faith, and remain anchored when circumstances shift. Declarations matter because words shape spiritual posture.

What we speak consistently is what we eventually believe, and what we believe governs how we respond to life. In moments of joy, declarations become praise. In moments of pressure, they become warfare. In moments of uncertainty, they become anchors of truth. Declaring God's Word aligns our hearts with heaven's perspective and positions us to see beyond what is visible to what is eternal.

Thanksgiving is emphasized as the gateway into God's presence. Gratitude shifts our focus from problems to promises, from fear to faith, from self to God. It recalibrates the soul and creates space for joy, peace, and trust to rise. When we enter with thanksgiving, we acknowledge that God is sovereign, good, and faithful regardless of what surrounds us. This posture of praise also grounds us in identity. We are reminded that the Lord is God, that He made us, and that we belong to Him. Declarations rooted in this truth silence doubt and reinforce confidence. We are not wandering alone; we are His people, securely kept as sheep in His pasture. His mercy is everlasting, and His truth endures across generations, making every declaration spoken in faith an investment beyond the present moment.

This book was prayerfully written to serve as a companion for believers seeking alignment, strength, healing, and confidence in God's Word. It is not intended to replace Scripture, but to help Scripture come alive through intentional declaration, reflection, and faith-filled prayer. Throughout these pages, God's Word is paired with encouragement and prayer designed to guide your heart into agreement with heaven. These declarations are rooted in the belief that God's Word is not only true but active. When spoken in faith, it shapes perspective, strengthens resolve, and positions the believer to walk confidently in God's promises. This book meets you wherever you are, whether in a season of waiting, restoration, breakthrough, or quiet trust, and invites you to slow down, speak deliberately, and allow God's truth to renew your mind and anchor your heart.

As you speak God's Word daily, whether in celebration or in challenge, may thanksgiving always lead the way. May your words continually usher you into the presence of the Lord, where strength is renewed, hope is restored, and faith is strengthened.

"Enter into his gates with thanksgiving, and into his courts with praise: be thankful unto him, and bless his name." Psalm 100:4

Table of Contents

INTRODUCTION

LIFE is lived in seasons, some marked by clarity and joy, others by waiting, pressure, uncertainty, or quiet endurance. In every season, God remains present, faithful, and actively involved, even when His work is not immediately visible.

Yet how we walk through these seasons is often shaped by what we believe, what we focus on, and what we choose to speak.

This book was created as a guide for believers who desire to walk intentionally with God through every circumstance of life. It is an invitation to engage God's Word not only as something to be read, but as something to be spoken, declared, and trusted daily. Throughout Scripture, God repeatedly reminds His people that His Word is living and powerful. When spoken in faith, it strengthens the heart, steadies the mind, and aligns the believer with heaven's truth.

Each section of this book centers on Scripture and addresses real-life experiences of fear and courage, waiting and fulfillment, strength and weakness, provision and trust, restoration and healing, protection and peace, obedience and elevation. These declarations are not abstract ideas or distant promises; they are God's truth applied to everyday life. They are meant to meet you where you are and lead you forward with clarity, hope, and confidence in God. This is not a book meant to be rushed. It is designed to be returned to again and again.

Some days, you may read one declaration slowly and allow it to settle deeply in your spirit. Other days, you may speak several aloud as an act of worship, warfare, or renewal. There is no pressure to keep pace, only an invitation to remain consistent, intentional, and anchored in truth.

As you move through these pages, you will notice a rhythm: Scripture, reflection, declaration, and prayer. This rhythm is intentional. It reflects a lifestyle of faith receiving God's Word, allowing it to shape understanding, speaking it with conviction, and responding to God in prayer. Over time, this practice builds spiritual confidence and cultivates a heart that remains steady regardless of circumstance.

Above all, this book is about alignment. Alignment with God's presence. Alignment with His promises. Alignment with His perspective. It is about choosing faith over fear, trust over anxiety, and truth over uncertainty. As you speak these declarations daily, may your heart grow more assured, your faith more grounded, and your walk with God more intentional.

May these words guide you into deeper trust, renewed strength, and lasting peace as you learn to live anchored, established, and confident in God's truth.

HOW TO USE
THIS BOOK

THIS book is designed to be spoken, not skimmed. It is a daily invitation to align your heart, your words, and your atmosphere with God's truth.

Begin with Thanksgiving

Before reading any declaration, pause and enter God's presence with gratitude. Thanksgiving is the gateway that prepares your spirit to receive and declare truth.

Read Aloud

Declarations carry power when spoken. Read slowly, intentionally, and with faith even when emotions have not yet caught up with truth.

Declare in Every Season

Use this book in moments of joy, waiting, uncertainty, or warfare. Declarations are not seasonal tools; they are a lifestyle.

Pause and Reflect

After each declaration, allow the Holy Spirit to highlight what applies to your current season. Let the Word settle in your spirit.

SCRIPTURE READING

Psalm 136:1–3 "O give thanks unto the LORD; for he is good: for his mercy endureth for ever. O give thanks unto the God of gods: for his mercy endureth for ever. O give thanks to the Lord of lords: for his mercy endureth for ever."

REFLECTION AND ENCOURAGEMENT

This psalm calls us into a holy rhythm of gratitude rooted in unchanging truth: God is good, and His mercy never ends. The repetition throughout Psalm 136 is intentional; it trains the heart to remember. When circumstances shift, emotions fluctuate, or seasons change, God's mercy remains constant. Psalm 136 reminds us that praise is not dependent on conditions. God's goodness is not seasonal, and His mercy does not wear out or run dry. Even when life feels uncertain, God's character stays the same. Thanksgiving becomes an act of faith, a declaration that God's goodness stands firm regardless of what surrounds you. Thanksgiving anchors the soul. It redirects attention away from what is lacking and centers it on who God is. When you give thanks, you acknowledge not only what God has done, but who He has always been faithful across generations, steady through every season, and merciful without end. This passage invites you to cultivate a lifestyle of praise. Not occasional gratitude, not reactive worship, but continual thanksgiving rooted in the everlasting mercy of God. Praise becomes your posture, and gratitude becomes your response.

A HEART OF

GRATITUDE!

PRAYER AND DAILY DECLARATION

HEAVENLY Father, I thank You for Your goodness and Your everlasting mercy. Your faithfulness has followed me through every season in times of clarity and in times of confusion, in abundance and in stretching. Not once has Your mercy failed me. Even when I did not fully recognize it, Your hand was sustaining me. Teach my heart to remain thankful not only when circumstances feel favorable, but in every moment. Guard me from selective gratitude. Let thanksgiving rise from a place of conviction, not convenience. When challenges arise, remind me that Your goodness does not change. When emotions fluctuate, anchor me in the constancy of Your mercy. Let praise continually rise from my spirit. Shape my thoughts with gratitude. Season my words with thanksgiving. Guide my actions with trust. May my life reflect an awareness of Your kindness and an expectation of Your continued faithfulness. Today, I decree and declare that the Lord is good. God's mercy endures forever. Thanksgiving fills my heart and my mouth. Praise anchors my faith daily. I live with gratitude, confidence, and trust. I will not forget Your works; I will not overlook Your mercy; I will not silence my praise. I choose to give thanks in all things, knowing that Your mercy remains constant, Your goodness is unshaken, and Your faithfulness surrounds my life. In Jesus mighty name, Amen

SCRIPTURE READING

Proverbs 18:21 "Death and life are in the power of the tongue: and they that love it shall eat the fruit thereof."

REFLECTION AND ENCOURAGEMENT

This verse reveals a profound spiritual principle: words are never neutral. Every word spoken carries direction, influence, and consequence. God has placed extraordinary power within your speech, the power to release life, healing, and hope, or to reinforce fear, defeat, and limitation. Your words shape atmospheres. They influence how you see yourself, how others are strengthened or discouraged, and how situations unfold over time. When your speech aligns with God's truth, faith rises, peace settles, and clarity emerges. Words spoken in wisdom become seeds that grow into fruit that reflects life, restoration, and purpose. God calls you to speak intentionally. This does not mean ignoring reality but choosing to frame it through faith. When challenges arise, your words can either magnify the problem or magnify God. The tongue becomes a tool of stewardship. What you speak today influences what you experience tomorrow. This passage invites you to maturity and mindfulness. As you submit your speech to God's Spirit, your words become instruments of grace. Life flows from your mouth, and good fruit follows those who choose wisdom in what they speak.

SPEAK LIFE DAILY!

PRAYER AND DAILY DECLARATION

HEAVENLY Father, I thank You for the authority You have placed in my words. You created the world through speech, and You have entrusted me with the ability to speak life, truth, and faith. Help me to recognize that my words carry influence over my heart, my environment, and those around me. Teach me to guard my tongue and align my speech with Your wisdom. Lord, purify my thoughts so that my words reflect truth and not fear. Remove careless speech, negativity, and doubt from my mouth. Let my language be seasoned with grace and governed by the Holy Spirit. When I am tempted to speak from frustration or emotion, pause my tongue and redirect my words toward faith and encouragement. Today, I decree and declare that my tongue speaks life and not death. My words align with God's truth and wisdom. My speech builds, heals, and strengthens. The Holy Spirit governs my conversations; faith fills my declarations. My words produce good and lasting fruit. What I speak carries peace and clarity. My mouth reflects the character of Christ. Let my words be intentional, my tone be gracious, and my declarations be rooted in faith. May my speech testify to Your wisdom at work within me and release blessing wherever I speak. In Jesus mighty name, Amen.

SCRIPTURE READING

REFLECTION AND ENCOURAGEMENT

This verse reveals the depth of God's intentional design over your life. Long before you were seen by people, you were known by God. Your existence was not accidental, delayed, or improvised. God formed you with purpose already in mind. "To know" in this context speaks of relationship and intention. God did not merely foresee you; He knew you. He set you apart before birth, marking your life with divine purpose. Sanctification here means consecration; your life was designated for God's use before you ever took a breath. Jeremiah 1:5 reminds you that your calling is not determined by age, background, mistakes, or current circumstance. God's assignment preceded all of that. Even when you feel unqualified or uncertain, God's word over your life remains unchanged. This passage invites you to rest in identity rather than performance. You are not trying to discover whether your life has meaning; your life was created with meaning. God is unfolding what He already established.

KNOWN BEFORE
I WAS FORMED!

PRAYER AND DAILY DECLARATION

HEAVENLY Father, I thank You that my life is not an accident. Before I was formed in my mother's womb, You knew me. Before I entered this world, You set me apart with intention and purpose. Thank You for creating me with divine wisdom and for establishing a plan for my life long before I understood it. Lord, help me to trust Your design over my life. When doubt, fear, or insecurity attempts to speak louder than Your truth, remind me that my identity and purpose are rooted in You. Strengthen my faith to believe that the One who called me will also equip and guide me. Teach me to walk in obedience and confidence, knowing that Your plans for me are good. Today, I decree and declare that I am known by God. I am chosen and set apart for a divine purpose. My life is ordained by God's will, and fear cannot cancel my calling. I walk confidently in the plan God has prepared for me. My steps are ordered, my purpose is secure, and my life is aligned with His wisdom. In Jesus mighty name, Amen.

SCRIPTURE READING

Psalm 23:1 "The LORD is my shepherd; I shall not want."

REFLECTION AND ENCOURAGEMENT

This verse is one of the most profound declarations of trust, care, and divine provision found in Scripture. To declare that the Lord is your Shepherd is to acknowledge His active and personal involvement in every area of your life. A shepherd does not abandon the sheep he watches, guides, corrects, protects, and provides with constant attention. In the same way, God is intimately involved in your journey, aware of your needs even before you ask. Because the Lord is your Shepherd, you are never without direction. Even when the path ahead feels uncertain or unfamiliar, He knows exactly where to lead you. His guidance brings peace to your decisions, clarity to your steps, and confidence to your heart. You are not wandering. You are being led deliberately by the One who sees the end from the beginning. The declaration "I shall not want" is not a denial of challenges; it is a proclamation of sufficiency. It speaks of freedom from lack, anxiety, and the fear of not having enough. God's provision reaches far beyond material needs. He supplies wisdom when decisions are difficult, strength when the journey feels long, peace when circumstances are noisy, and rest when your soul is weary, trusting God as your Shepherd shifts your posture from striving to resting. You are invited to release control and lean into His faithful care. Your life is sustained not by effort alone, but by the steady, intentional provision of a loving God who ensures that what you need arrives at the right time, in the right measure, for the right purpose.

THE LORD IS MY SHEPHERD!

PRAYER AND DAILY DECLARATION

HEAVENLY Father, I thank You for being my Shepherd and for watching over my life with love, wisdom, and faithfulness. I acknowledge that You are my source, my guide, and my provider in every season. You see the path ahead of me, and You lead me with care and purpose. Thank You for the assurance that I am never alone, never forgotten, and never without Your direction. Lord, help me to trust Your guidance even when the way forward is not fully clear. Teach my heart to rest in Your leadership and to follow Your voice with confidence. Where worry or uncertainty tries to take hold, fill my heart with peace and assurance that You are faithfully caring for every detail of my life. Today, I decree and declare that the Lord is my Shepherd, and I am divinely guided. I lack nothing that God has ordained for my life. I am led in peace, provision, and protection. My needs are supplied according to God's perfect care, and my life is sustained by His faithful hand. I choose to rest in Your guidance and depend fully on Your provision. Lead me, sustain me, and keep me in every season. I release anxiety and embrace trust, knowing that my Shepherd watches over me with unfailing love. In Jesus mighty name, Amen.

SCRIPTURE READING

Isaiah 43:18–19 "Remember ye not the former things, neither consider the things of old. Behold, I will do a new thing; now it shall spring forth; shall ye not know it? I will even make a way in the wilderness, and rivers in the desert."

REFLECTION AND ENCOURAGEMENT

These verses carry a powerful invitation to release the past and embrace what God is unfolding. God does not deny former seasons, but He instructs you not to live anchored to them. What has been is not meant to limit what He is about to do. God declares, "I will do a new thing." This is not a recycled blessing or a repeated pattern; it is fresh, intentional, and timely. The new thing may begin quietly, but it carries divine momentum. God asks, "Shall ye not know it?" reminding you to stay spiritually alert so you do not miss what He is birthing. Wilderness and desert represent places of lack, delay, or difficulty. Yet God promises to create pathways where none existed and supply where resources seemed impossible. His power is not restricted by the environment. What looks barren becomes a place of breakthrough when God intervenes. Isaiah 43:18–19 encourages you to shift expectation. The future is not blocked by the past. God is actively working, creating access, restoring hope, and releasing new life where you least expect it.

GOD IS DOING
A NEW THING!

PRAYER AND DAILY DECLARATION

HEAVENLY Father, I thank You for being a God of new beginnings. I release former seasons, disappointments, and limitations into Your hands. I choose not to live anchored to what was but aligned with what You are doing now. Open my eyes to recognize the new thing You are bringing forth. Make a way where I see none. Let rivers flow into the dry places of my life. Renew my hope and strengthen my faith as I trust You for a breakthrough. Today, I decree and declare that God is doing a new thing in my life. My past does not limit my future. God makes a way in impossible places. I decree and declare that dry places are filled with divine supply. I walk forward with renewed hope and faith. I step into the new season, You have prepared expectant, confident, and trusting the God who makes all things new. In Jesus mighty name, Amen.

SCRIPTURE READING

Psalm 5:11–12 "But let all those that put their trust in thee rejoice: let them ever shout for joy, because thou defendest them: let them also that love thy name be joyful in thee. For thou, LORD, wilt bless the righteous; with favour wilt thou compass him as with a shield."

REFLECTION AND ENCOURAGEMENT

This passage reveals the joy and security found in trusting God. Those who place their trust in Him are invited not merely to be glad, but to rejoice openly and continually. Their joy is rooted in the assurance that God Himself is their defender. Praise rises naturally when the heart rests in divine protection. Psalm 5 reminds us that joy is a response to trust. When you know God surrounds you, fear loses its grip and praise finds its voice. God's defense is not passive; it is active and intentional. He watches, guards, and preserves those who love His name. The imagery of favor as a shield is powerful. A shield surrounds, protects, and absorbs what would otherwise cause harm. God's favor is not distant or abstract; it encircles the righteous, covering them in every direction. His blessing is not fragile; it is enduring and secure. Let this passage encourage you to rejoice, even before the outcome is fully visible. Trust in God produces joy, and joy strengthens faith. When you rest in His defense, your life becomes a testimony of praise and confidence in His favor.

DIVINELY
COVERED ALWAYS

PRAYER AND DAILY DECLARATION

HEAVENLY Father, I thank You for being my defender and my shield. You are my covering, my protection, and my peace. When opposition rises, I will not fear, because You stand between me and every attack. My trust is anchored in who You are, not in what I see. Teach me to rely fully on You. Let my trust produce unshakable joy and steady confidence. Remove anxiety and doubt, and replace them with bold faith. Father, clothe me in boldness. Remove every trace of anxiety, hesitation, or doubt. Where fear once tried to settle, let faith arise. Where heaviness tried to linger, let praise overflow. I choose joy as an act of faith. I choose confidence as a declaration of trust. I choose praise as a weapon of victory. Where heaviness tries to linger, let praise rise. I choose joy as an act of faith, and I choose confidence as a declaration of trust. Surround me with Your favor as a shield. Let Your blessing rest upon my life, my household, and every assignment connected to me. Establish my steps in peace and purpose as I walk boldly in Your presence. Today, I decree and declare that My trust in God produces joy. The Lord is my defender and my shield. I am divinely protected and surrounded by favor. Blessing rests upon my life. I rejoice in the Lord always. I stand confident, covered, and victorious. In Jesus mighty name, Amen.

SCRIPTURE READING

Isaiah 41:10–14   "Do not be afraid, I am with you! I am your God, let nothing terrify you! I will make you strong and help you; I will protect you and save you. Those who are angry with you will know the shame of defeat. Those who fight against you will disappear from the earth. I am the LORD your God; I strengthen you and say, 'Do not be afraid; I will help you. 'Small and weak as you are, do not be afraid; I will help you. I, the Holy One of Israel, am the one who saves you."

REFLECTION AND ENCOURAGEMENT

This passage is a powerful reassurance from God spoken directly into moments of fear, uncertainty, and weakness. God does not ignore the reality of struggle, but He answers it with the greater truth of His presence. The command "Do not be afraid" is not rooted in human strength, but in the promise that God Himself is near. When He declares, "I am with you," fear begins to lose its hold. God identifies Himself personally: "I am your God." This covenant language reminds you that you are not abandoned or left to navigate life alone. From this relationship flows His promise of strength, help, protection, and salvation. Even when you feel small or inadequate, God's assurance remains steady. His help does not depend on your ability but on His faithfulness. What rises against you will not endure. The Holy One of Israel stands as your Redeemer and Defender. He strengthens your hands, steadies your heart, and calls you to move forward with confidence, knowing that His presence surrounds and sustains you.

THE LORD LEADS MY LIFE!

PRAYER AND DAILY DECLARATION

HEAVENLY Father, I thank You for Your reassuring presence in my life. You see my fears, You know my weaknesses, and yet You speak strength, help, and victory over me. I choose to trust You completely. Today, I decree and declare that I will not be afraid, for the Lord my God is with me, and I am strengthened by God's power and upheld by His righteous hand. I decree and declare that fear, anxiety, doubt, and confusion have no authority over my life; I walk in courage, faith, and divine confidence. I decree and declare that every opposition rising against me is defeated and dismantled by God's power. No weapon formed against me shall prosper. I am helped, protected, preserved, and victorious. Even in moments of weakness, I am empowered by heaven. Today, I decree and declare that the Holy One of Israel is my Redeemer and Defender. I rise, move forward, and fulfill destiny without fear. I rest in Your promises, trust in Your help, and walk boldly knowing You are with me. In Jesus mighty name, Amen.

SCRIPTURE READING

Philippians 4:13 "I can do all things through Christ, which strengtheneth me."

REFLECTION AND ENCOURAGEMENT

This scripture is a powerful declaration of where true strength is found. It reminds you that your ability to endure, overcome, and succeed does not originate from your own capacity, experience, or resources, but it flows directly from Christ. When your strength feels insufficient, Christ becomes more than enough. Life will present moments that stretch you beyond what feels comfortable or manageable. There will be seasons when responsibility feels heavy, challenges seem unending, and confidence begins to waver. In those moments, this verse anchors your heart in an unchanging truth: Christ supplies strength that does not run out. His strength is not emotional, circumstantial, or temporary; it is constant and sustaining. Apostle Paul's declaration was born from experience, not ease. He learned that Christ's strength is present in every condition, whether in abundance or lack, certainty or uncertainty. This means your current season does not disqualify you. Instead, it becomes the very place where Christ's power is revealed most clearly through you. Through Christ, you are not merely surviving; you are equipped to rise, endure, and move forward with purpose. His strength enables you to push past fear, remain steady under pressure, and walk boldly in obedience to God's call. Nothing assigned to you is too great when Christ is the source sustaining you. What feels impossible in your own power becomes achievable when you rely fully on Him.

MY PORTION IS ASSIGNED BY GOD!

PRAYER AND DAILY DECLARATION

HEAVENLY Father, I thank You that my portion in life is divinely assigned and not randomly determined. You have measured out my steps with wisdom and intention. The responsibilities, opportunities, and callings before me are not accidents. They are appointed by You. And where You assign, You also supply. I acknowledge that my strength does not come from my own ability, but from Christ who lives within me. Apart from You, I can do nothing; yet through Christ, I am fully equipped, sustained, and empowered for every assignment You place before me. I refuse to measure my capacity by my feelings or limitations. I measure it by Your grace at work in me. Today, I decree and declare that Christ strengthens me in all that I do. My portion is matched with sufficient grace. I am not limited by fear, weakness, or doubt. Divine wisdom guides my decisions. Endurance sustains me through every season. Every assignment before me is achievable through His strength. I am equipped for what I have been called to carry. God's power works effectively within me. Lord, I rely on Your strength daily. Sustain me when I feel weary. Guide me when I feel uncertain. Carry me through seasons of stretching and growth. I step forward assured, capable, and bold, knowing that the God who assigned my portion also empowers me to fulfill it. In Jesus mighty name, Amen.

SCRIPTURE READING

REFLECTION AND ENCOURAGEMENT

These verses proclaim God's unmistakable promise of divine protection in the midst of danger and uncertainty. They acknowledge the reality that adversity may exist around you, chaos may unfold, challenges may arise, and threats may appear. Still, they boldly declare that none of these has permission to cross the boundary God has placed over your life. God's protection is not random or accidental. It is intentional, covenant-based, and rooted in relationship. To dwell under His shadow is to live with a conscious awareness of His presence, authority, and care. While others may be affected by turmoil, God preserves those who trust in Him, shielding them from harm and sustaining them through every season. This message also reveals that protection does not always mean the absence of trouble; it means distinction within it. You may witness difficulty, loss, or judgment around you, yet remain untouched by its impact. God allows you to stand securely while He reveals His justice, faithfulness, and sovereignty. God invites you to rest in confidence rather than fear. You are not exposed, vulnerable, or forgotten; you are covered. God stands as your refuge and fortress, ensuring that what threatens others does not overpower you. His covering brings peace to your heart, courage to your steps, and assurance that your life is firmly held in His hands.

DIVINELY PROTECTED!

PRAYER AND DAILY DECLARATION

HEAVENLY Father, I thank You for being my refuge, my defender, and my strong tower. You are my place of safety in every season. When uncertainty surrounds me, You remain constant. When adversity arises You stand as my shield. I rest in the assurance that You have placed a divine boundary around my life and my household, a boundary no force of darkness can cross. Lord, I trust completely in Your preserving power. Guard my steps as I go out and as I come in. Cover my dwelling with Your peace. Let Your angels encamp around me and let Your presence distinguish me from destruction. Even in the midst of adversity, I am not vulnerable; I am covered. I am not exposed, I am hidden in You. Today, I decree and declare I am divinely protected on every side. No harm shall come near me or my household. God's covering distinguishes me from destruction. I am preserved in the midst of adversity. I walk in safety, confidence, and supernatural peace. The Lord guards my steps and secures my dwelling. My heart is settled. My spirit is at rest. My life is preserved by the mighty power of God. In Jesus mighty name, Amen.

SCRIPTURE READING

Romans 8:28 "And we know that all things work together for good to them that love God, to them who are called according to his purpose."

REFLECTION AND ENCOURAGEMENT

This verse is a deep well of comfort, assurance, and perspective for every believer. It reminds you that God is not reacting to your life. He is intentionally orchestrating it. Nothing you have walked through, whether joyful or painful, has escaped His attention or fallen outside His redemptive plan. There are seasons when God's hand feels obvious and others when His work seems hidden. Yet this scripture reassures you that even the moments that confuse you are being woven together with purpose. God does not waste experiences. He redeems them. What once felt like loss becomes preparation. What felt like a delay becomes alignment. What felt like disappointment becomes direction. This promise is anchored in relationship and calling. It is for those who love God and are walking according to His purpose. That means every detail of your life, both the celebrated and the unseen, is being aligned toward good. Not always comfort, but growth. Not always easy, but fulfillment. God is shaping your character, strengthening your faith, and positioning you for the future He has ordained. When this truth settles in your heart, fear loosens its grip. You are free to move forward with hope and confidence, knowing that God is actively working behind the scenes. Your story is not random. It is intentional, purposeful, and guided by a faithful God who brings beauty out of every chapter.

ALL THINGS WORK FOR GOOD!

PRAYER AND DAILY DECLARATION

HEAVENLY Father, I thank You that You are intentional, purposeful, and unfailingly faithful. You are never careless with my life. Even in seasons I do not fully understand, You are actively working behind the scenes, aligning circumstances, refining my character, and positioning me according to Your divine plan. Nothing escapes Your awareness, and nothing is outside Your control. Lord, help me trust You beyond what I see. When answers seem delayed, and the path feels unclear, anchor my heart in the truth that You are weaving every detail together for my good. Remind me that no season is wasted, no delay is accidental, and no experience is in vain. What I perceive as detours are often divine redirections. What makes me feel like waiting is often preparation. Today, I decree and declare, All things are working together for my good. God's purpose is being fulfilled in my life. Every season serves a divine assignment. I am aligned with heaven's timing and direction. My steps are ordered by the Lord. I walk in faith, hope, and divine alignment. I choose to trust You completely past, present, and future. Strengthen my heart to rest confidently in Your promises. Give me the courage to walk boldly in the calling You have placed upon my life. Let my life reflect Your wisdom, Your timing, and Your perfect plan. In Jesus mighty name, Amen.

SCRIPTURE READING

REFLECTION AND ENCOURAGEMENT

This verse reveals the source of true strength. God does not merely strengthen circumstances. He strengthens you. The prayer in Ephesians 3:16 points inward, reminding us that lasting endurance begins within the inner man. God's strength is not measured by human capacity or emotional energy. It is released "according to the riches of His glory," meaning it is abundant, limitless, and sufficient for every season. When external pressures feel heavy, God fortifies the heart, stabilizes the mind, and renews the spirit through His Spirit. The "inner man" represents your core, your faith, resolve, and spiritual foundation. When God strengthens you there, you are not easily shaken by outward challenges. You gain resilience, courage, and quiet confidence that does not depend on circumstances changing. Ephesians 3:16 reassures you that weakness is not a dead end; it is an invitation for divine empowerment. God strengthens you from the inside out so you can stand, endure, and move forward with grace and confidence.

STRENGTHENED

FROM WITHIN!

PRAYER AND DAILY DECLARATION

HEAVENLY Father, I thank You for the sustaining strength You provide through Your Spirit. When I feel weak, overwhelmed, or stretched beyond my natural ability, You do not leave me unsupported. You strengthen me from within. Your power is not distant; it is alive and active in my inner being, renewing, restoring, and establishing me. Lord, fortify my heart where it has grown weary. Strengthen my faith where it has been tested. Steady my emotions where pressure has tried to shake me. Let Your Spirit infuse me with supernatural endurance and quiet confidence. When fear attempts to whisper, let Your power rise louder. When challenges press in, let Your strength rise within me. I receive Your divine empowerment today. Not just physical strength, but spiritual resilience. Not just temporary motivation, but lasting inner renewal. Anchor me deeply in You so that I am not moved by circumstances, criticism, pressure, or uncertainty. Today, I decree and declare: I am strengthened by God's Spirit. My inner man is renewed with divine power. God's strength sustains me daily. I am not moved by pressure or fear. I stand firm, steady, and spiritually fortified. The power of God works mightily within me. I move forward renewed, empowered, and established. I endure with grace. I trust with confidence. I overcome through divine strength. In Jesus mighty name, Amen.

SCRIPTURE READING

2 Timothy 1:7 "For God hath not given us the spirit of fear; but of power, and of love, and of a sound mind."

REFLECTION AND ENCOURAGEMENT

This verse clearly defines what does and does not come from God. Fear is not a gift from Him. Anxiety, intimidation, and paralysis are not evidence of God's presence; they are signals to return to truth. God replaces fear with power, love, and a sound mind. Power speaks of divine strength and authority, the ability to stand firm, move forward, and act boldly even when circumstances are challenging. Love anchors that power, ensuring that our actions are rooted in compassion, grace, and selflessness. A sound mind brings clarity, stability, and discernment, guarding the heart from chaos and confusion. 2 Timothy 1:7 reminds us that fear is not meant to govern our decisions or define our future. God equips His people with inner strength, emotional balance, and spiritual confidence. When fear attempts to rise, this verse calls us to remember what God has already placed within us. Let this truth reassure you: you are not weak, overwhelmed, or abandoned. You are empowered by God, guided by love, and sustained by a disciplined, sound mind. Fear has no authority where God's Spirit reigns.

POWER, LOVE, SOUND MIND!

PRAYER AND DAILY DECLARATION

HEAVENLY Father, I thank You that fear does not originate from You. It is not my inheritance, and it is not my portion. You have not created me to live intimidated, anxious, or restrained. Through Your Spirit, You have equipped me with power, love, and a sound mind. What You have placed within me is greater than any fear that attempts to confront me. Lord, expose and uproot every subtle form of fear: fear of failure, fear of rejection, fear of the unknown, fear of delay, fear of lack. Replace it with bold faith and quiet confidence. When anxious thoughts try to arise, let Your truth silence them. When confusion attempts to cloud my judgment, let Your wisdom bring clarity. Let Your love govern my responses and shape my decisions. Teach me to respond from a place of security, not insecurity; from assurance, not anxiety. Guard my mind with Your peace. Establish my thoughts in truth. Align my emotions with faith. Today, I decree and declare: Fear has no hold over my life. I walk in God-given power and authority. Love directs my actions and decisions. My mind is sound, focused, and disciplined. Peace guards my thoughts and steadies my heart. I choose clarity over confusion and faith over fear. I live boldly. I stand confidently. I move forward unshaken. I embrace the identity You have given me. In Jesus mighty name, Amen.

SCRIPTURE READING

REFLECTION AND ENCOURAGEMENT

This verse is a gentle yet powerful reminder that God is intentional about every detail of your life. The "lines" represent boundaries, portions, and assignments that God has carefully measured out for you according to His wisdom and love. Nothing about your life is accidental. Where you are, what you carry, and what has been entrusted to you are all part of God's deliberate design. To say that the lines have fallen in "pleasant places" is not to deny challenges or growth seasons. Rather, it affirms that even within boundaries, God's goodness is present. What He has allotted to you is sufficient, purposeful, and marked with His favor. Your portion may still be unfolding, but it is already secure in God's hands. This verse also reorients the heart toward gratitude. When you recognize that your heritage comes from the Lord, comparison loses its grip. You begin to see that your path does not need to resemble someone else's to be meaningful. God's wisdom shaped your journey, your timing, and your inheritance uniquely for you. A "goodly heritage" speaks not only of material provision, but of spiritual legacy, peace, purpose, and future hope. God has established something valuable through your life, something worth stewarding with gratitude and trust. As you embrace your portion, you step confidently into a future filled with God's goodness and intentional care.

PLEASANT PLACES ESTABLISHED!

PRAYER AND DAILY DECLARATION

HEAVENLY Father, I thank You for the portion You have wisely and intentionally assigned to me. You are not random with my life. You have ordered my steps with precision, purpose, and love. The boundaries You have drawn around me are not limitations; they are divine assignments filled with protection, provision, and promise. I receive my heritage with gratitude, knowing that what You have given me is good, fitting, and aligned with my destiny. Lord, free my heart from comparison. Remove every desire to measure my life against another's journey. Teach me to celebrate the grace You have uniquely placed upon me. Let gratitude silence discontent and trust silence doubt. Help me see my portion not through temporary emotion, but through eternal perspective. You are the One who establishes my inheritance. You secure my future and sustain my present. Even in seasons that stretch me, I trust that the lines have fallen to me in pleasant places. What You have assigned to me carries goodness, growth, and divine favor. Nothing about my life is accidental. Every boundary holds a blessing. Every season carries purpose. Today, I decree and declare: The lines have fallen to me in pleasant places. I have a goodly heritage from the Lord. My portion is blessed, secure, and purposeful. Comparison has no place in my heart. Gratitude governs my perspective. My future is filled with God's goodness and favor. I choose contentment. I choose trust. I choose Thanksgiving. My steps are confident. My heart is anchored. My inheritance is established by the Lord. In Jesus mighty name, Amen.

SCRIPTURE READING

REFLECTION AND ENCOURAGEMENT

This verse reveals the posture that sustains a vibrant and victorious spiritual life. Prayer is not meant to be occasional or reactive; it is meant to be continual. To "continue in prayer" speaks of consistency, devotion, and relationship. God invites you into an ongoing dialogue with Him—one that is not driven by urgency alone, but by trust, dependence, and intimacy. Apostle Paul pairs prayer with watchfulness, reminding believers to remain spiritually alert and discerning. Watchfulness is the awareness of God's movement, the sensitivity to His voice, and the readiness to respond when He leads. It guards your heart from distraction, complacency, and spiritual dullness. A watchful spirit keeps you aligned with God's purposes and attentive to His instruction. Thanksgiving anchors this posture. Gratitude shifts prayer from anxiety to assurance. When thanksgiving accompanies prayer, it strengthens faith and reinforces trust in God's faithfulness. Gratitude acknowledges what God has already done while expecting what He is yet to do. It keeps your heart steady, hopeful, and grounded in truth. This verse teaches that prayer is not just communication; it is cultivation. Through continual prayer, watchfulness, and thanksgiving, your spiritual life remains nourished, focused, and resilient. You are strengthened to stand firm, discern clearly, and move forward with peace. A prayerful and grateful life keeps you connected to heaven's perspective and anchored in God's sustaining grace.

STEADFAST IN PRAYER!

PRAYER AND DAILY DECLARATION

HEAVENLY Father, I thank You for calling me into a life of continual prayer and spiritual awareness. You have not invited me into a distant relationship, but into daily communion a steady, ongoing connection that sustains my faith and anchors my heart. Teach me to remain connected to You in every season, every moment, and every circumstance, whether in abundance or in uncertainty. Lord, cultivate in me a steadfast and disciplined prayer life. Let prayer become my first response, not my last resort. Sharpen my spiritual sensitivity so that my spirit remains alert, discerning, and responsive to Your leading. Guard me from distraction, complacency, and spiritual dullness. Help me to recognize Your voice clearly and to follow Your direction with confidence and obedience. Let thanksgiving govern my heart. Remove anxiety, restlessness, and doubt, and replace them with gratitude and assurance. When I pray, let faith rise within me. When I watch, let wisdom guide me. When I give thanks, let confidence in Your faithfulness steady my soul. Gratitude anchors me in truth and reminds me that You are already at work on my behalf. Today, I decree and declare I am steadfast and consistent in prayer. My spirit remains alert and spiritually aware. Thanksgiving governs my heart and strengthens my faith. Anxiety has no hold over me. Peace guards my mind and steadies my steps. I am aligned with God's will and attentive to His direction. In Jesus mighty name, Amen.

SCRIPTURE READING

Hebrews 5:14 "But strong meat belongeth to them that are of full age, even those who by reason of use have their senses exercised to discern both good and evil."

REFLECTION AND ENCOURAGEMENT

This verse speaks to spiritual maturity, the kind that develops through consistent practice, obedience, and time spent walking with God. Spiritual growth is not measured only by knowledge, but by discernment. Mature believers are trained to recognize what aligns with God and what does not. Hebrews 5:14 reminds us that discernment is developed "by reason of use." It is cultivated through daily application of God's Word, choosing obedience repeatedly, and allowing truth to shape decisions. Growth happens when faith is exercised, not merely admired. "Strong meat" represents a deeper understanding of wisdom that sustains in complex seasons. God desires to grow you beyond surface-level faith into stability, clarity, and confidence. As you mature, your spiritual senses sharpen. You become less reactive and more discerning. Less confused and more grounded. This passage encourages patience with the process of growth. Maturity is formed, not rushed. God is training your discernment so that you can walk wisely, choose well, and remain steady in every season.

MATURITY THROUGH DISCERNMENT!

PRAYER AND DAILY DECLARATION

HEAVENLY Father, I thank You for Your desire to grow me into spiritual maturity. You are not content to leave me where I started; You are shaping my character, deepening my understanding, and strengthening my faith. Thank You for forming me through Your Word and through the quiet work of Your Spirit within me. Lord, sharpen my discernment and strengthen my spiritual understanding. Train my heart to recognize what is good, true, and pleasing to You. Guard me from deception, distraction, and decisions driven by emotion rather than truth. Let Your Word be the standard that guides every thought, choice, and opportunity in my life. Help me grow beyond surface faith into steady confidence. When challenges arise, let maturity guide my response. When decisions must be made, let wisdom lead me. Form within me a stable and discerning heart that is not easily shaken or misled. Today, I decree and declare that I am growing in spiritual maturity. God's Word sharpens my discernment, and wisdom governs my decisions. Clarity replaces confusion, and I am led by truth rather than impulse. My faith is deep, steady, and established. God is completing the good work He has begun in me, and I move forward grounded, discerning, and confident in Him. In Jesus mighty name, Amen.

SCRIPTURE READING

REFLECTION AND ENCOURAGEMENT

This verse is a tender yet powerful promise from God to those who have been wounded physically, emotionally, or relationally. God does not ignore pain that comes from rejection, neglect, or abandonment. He speaks directly to it with intention: "I will restore health unto thee." Restoration here means more than relief; it means repair. God does not simply cover wounds. He heals them. What others labeled as "outcast" did not change God's view or His plan. Human rejection never cancels divine attention. Where people withdrew care, God steps in with compassion and authority. Jeremiah 30:17 reassures you that God responds personally to pain that was unjustly inflicted. He sees the source of the wound and addresses it directly. Shame, isolation, and rejection do not get the final word; God does. This promise invites you to release the identity formed by hurtful labels and embrace God's restoring truth. You are not forgotten. You are not discarded. You are seen, valued, and healed by the Lord Himself.

DIVINE RESTORATION

IS RELEASED!

PRAYER AND DAILY DECLARATION

HEAVENLY Father, I thank You for being the God who restores, heals, and makes all things new. You are not indifferent to my pain. You see every wound, those that are visible and those hidden deep within my heart. Nothing escapes Your compassion, and nothing is beyond Your restoring power. Where there has been loss, You bring renewal. Where there has been damage, You bring repair. Lord, I receive Your healing touch over my body, my mind, my emotions, and my spirit. Restore strength where weakness has lingered. Restore clarity where confusion once settled. Restore joy where sorrow attempted to take root. Where rejection tried to define my identity, reaffirm who You say I am, chosen, loved, and accepted. Where neglect or disappointment left scars, pour out Your wholeness and peace. You are the God who does not merely patch what is broken. You rebuild, renew, and redeem. I trust You to restore completely, not partially. Heal what was wounded by words, by circumstances, or by seasons of hardship. Let restoration reach every area of my life, my health, my relationships, my confidence, and my purpose. Today, I decree and declare God restores my health and renews my strength. Every wound is healed by the Lord. Rejection does not define me; God's love does. Restoration is active and working in my life. What was broken is being rebuilt. What was lost is being restored according to God's goodness. I am whole. I am valued. I am renewed. I walk forward healed, restored, and confident, upheld by the faithful and tender care of my God. In Jesus mighty name, Amen.

SCRIPTURE READING

REFLECTION AND ENCOURAGEMENT

This verse reveals a powerful kingdom principle: mercy flows in cycles. What you extend outward returns inward. Mercy is not weakness; it is strength under control, compassion in action, and grace expressed through love. Jesus teaches that mercy positions the heart to receive. When you choose mercy, you align yourself with God's character. You reflect His patience, His kindness, and His willingness to forgive and restore. Mercy softens the heart and keeps it responsive to God's work. Matthew 5:7 reassures you that God sees every act of compassion, every moment you choose understanding over judgment, forgiveness over offense, love over resentment. Mercy does not go unnoticed. It is met with mercy from God Himself. This passage invites you to live freely. When mercy governs your heart, you are not weighed down by bitterness or retaliation. You remain open to healing, restoration, and blessing.

MERCY GIVEN, MERCY RECEIVED!

PRAYER AND DAILY DECLARATION

HEAVENLY Father, I thank You for the immeasurable gift of Your mercy. Your compassion meets me daily, not because I have earned it, but because You are gracious and kind. You see my weaknesses, my shortcomings, and my struggles, yet You respond with patience and love. Thank You for not dealing with me according to my mistakes, but according to Your mercy. Today, I receive Your compassion fully and without hesitation. Where guilt has tried to linger, let mercy speak louder. Where shame has attempted to hold me back, let Your forgiveness set me free. Cleanse my heart and remind me that I stand accepted, covered, and restored by Your grace. Lord, shape my heart to reflect the mercy You have shown me. Where hurt has tempted me toward hardness, soften me. Where offense has lingered, give me the courage to release forgiveness. Guard me from bitterness and teach me to respond with grace. Let mercy flow through my words, my actions, and my decisions. May compassion guide my responses, even when it costs me pride. Today, I decree and declare I walk in mercy and compassion. I receive God's mercy freely and fully. Forgiveness frees my heart from bitterness. Mercy opens doors of blessing in my life. I am not bound by offense. I am not ruled by resentment. I am shaped by grace and anchored in peace. As I extend mercy, I experience mercy. As I forgive, I remain free. My life reflects the kindness and compassion of my faithful God. In Jesus mighty name, Amen.

SCRIPTURE READING

Proverbs 3:5 "Trust in the LORD with all thine heart; and lean not unto thine own understanding."

REFLECTION AND ENCOURAGEMENT

This verse calls you into a posture of full reliance on God. Trusting the Lord with all your heart means placing confidence not partially, but completely, in His wisdom, character, and faithfulness. It is an invitation to rest your weight on God rather than on your own reasoning. Leaning on your own understanding often feels safer because it is familiar. But God reminds you that human perspective is limited. What you see is only part of the picture. God sees the whole. When you release the need to figure everything out, you create space for God to guide you with clarity and peace. Proverbs 3:5 reassures you that trust is not blind; it is anchored in who God is. He has proven Himself faithful across generations. Trusting Him does not mean you ignore wisdom or responsibility; it means you acknowledge that God's wisdom is higher than yours. This verse invites you to surrender control. You are not required to have all the answers. God is asking for your heart, not your certainty. When trust replaces self-reliance, peace follows.

CONFIDENCE BEYOND UNDERSTANDING!

PRAYER AND DAILY DECLARATION

HEAVENLY Father, I choose to trust You with all my heart, not partially, not conditionally, but completely. Even when circumstances are unclear and outcomes are uncertain, I surrender my need to control and my desire to understand every detail. I place my plans, my questions, and my concerns into Your capable and faithful hands. Teach me to rely on Your wisdom above my own reasoning. Where my understanding is limited, remind me that Yours is infinite. Where I see fragments, You see the full picture. Strengthen me to trust beyond what is visible and to believe beyond what is explainable. When uncertainty rises, let trust rise higher. When fear attempts to settle, anchor my heart firmly in Your unchanging faithfulness. Lord, quiet every anxious thought that demands answers before obedience. Help me rest in the assurance that You are ordering my steps with intention and care. You are not confused about my future, and You are never late in fulfilling Your promises. I choose to lean into Your guidance and walk in yielded confidence. Today, I decree and declare that I trust the Lord with all my heart. I do not lean on my own understanding. God's wisdom directs my steps. Peace replaces anxiety in my mind. Clarity comes as I follow His leading. My heart is fully surrendered to God. I am secure in His plan. I am confident in His timing. I am steady in faith, even without full explanation. I walk forward trusting, yielding, and established, confident that the Lord is faithfully leading me into His perfect will. In Jesus mighty name, Amen.

SCRIPTURE READING

Psalm 51:17 "The sacrifices of God are a broken spirit: a broken and a contrite heart, O God, thou wilt not despise."

REFLECTION AND ENCOURAGEMENT

This verse reveals what God values most, not outward performance, but inward posture. A broken and contrite heart is not one crushed by shame; it is a heart softened by truth, humility, and repentance. God is not drawn to perfection. He is drawn to sincerity. David teaches us that God does not reject honesty. When your heart comes before Him, aware, repentant, and open, God does not turn away. He draws near. Brokenness here speaks of surrender, the release of pride, self-justification, and resistance. Contrition speaks of alignment, a heart willing to be shaped by God's mercy. Psalm 51:17 reassures you that God never despises humility. Even when you feel weak, undone, or aware of your need, you are not rejected. In fact, this posture creates space for restoration, healing, and renewal. God meets you exactly where you are. This verse invites you to come as you are, honest, yielded, and trusting. God's response to humility is grace.

RESTORED THROUGH SURRENDER!

PRAYER AND DAILY DECLARATION

HEAVENLY Father, I come before You with a humble and surrendered heart. I lay aside pride, self-reliance, and every attempt to appear strong, choosing honesty and surrender instead. You see me fully, my weaknesses, failures, and hidden struggles, yet You respond with mercy and compassion. Thank You for drawing near to the brokenhearted and restoring those who come to You sincerely. Create in me a clean heart, O God, and renew a right spirit within me. Purify my motives and align my desires with Your will. Teach me to walk in humility, not as weakness, but as strength rooted in dependence on You. Soften my heart, make me sensitive to Your voice, and willing to receive Your correction. Today, I decree and declare that God receives my humble and contrite heart. Repentance draws me closer to His presence. Pride has no authority over my life, and humility positions me for grace and growth. God restores and renews my spirit. I am forgiven, restored, and made whole. I rise from brokenness stronger and anchored in His mercy. In Jesus mighty name, Amen.

SCRIPTURE READING

Galatians 4:19 "My little children, of whom I travail in birth again until Christ be formed in you,"

REFLECTION AND ENCOURAGEMENT

This verse reveals the heart of spiritual formation. Apostle Paul speaks with deep love and intensity, describing spiritual growth as a process that requires care, patience, and perseverance. To have Christ formed in you is not a surface change; it is an inward transformation that reshapes desires, character, and identity. Formation takes time. Just as natural growth cannot be rushed, spiritual maturity develops through seasons of learning, correction, surrender, and obedience. God is not only interested in what you do for Him. He is deeply invested in who you are becoming in Him. Galatians 4:19 reminds you that God's goal is Christlikeness. He desires that the life of Christ be evident in your thoughts, responses, attitudes, and choices. This formation happens through the work of the Holy Spirit as you yield daily to God's truth. If growth feels uncomfortable at times, this verse reassures you that it is purposeful. God is shaping you with intention. What He is forming within you will be lasting, authentic, and reflective of Christ.

TRANSFORMED INTO HIS LIKENESS!

PRAYER AND DAILY DECLARATION

HEAVENLY Father, I thank You for Your faithful and intentional work in my life. You are shaping me daily into the likeness of Christ. I willingly surrender to Your transforming process. Form Christ within me. Shape my heart to reflect His humility, compassion, obedience, and love. Renew my mind so that my thoughts align with Your truth. Purify my desires so that what I long for reflects Your will. Where old patterns resist Your work, remove them. Where pride rises, replace it with humility. Where selfishness lingers, cultivate selflessness. Lord, when growth feels stretching or uncomfortable, give me grace to remain yielded. Teach me to trust the process of refinement. Let conviction lead to change and let discipline produce maturity. I do not want surface change; I desire a deep transformation that reaches my character, my speech, my reactions, and my decisions. Let my life increasingly reflect the character of Christ in how I love, how I forgive, how I serve, and how I respond under pressure. May others see not just my effort, but the evidence of Your Spirit at work within me. Today, I decree and declare Christ is being formed in me. My life is shaped by God's truth. Transformation is active and continual within me. My mind is being renewed daily. I am growing in spiritual maturity and depth. My character reflects Christ more each day. I remain surrendered. I remain teachable. I remain confident in God's refining work. The One who began a good work in me is faithful to complete it. I walk forward transformed, aligned, and steadily becoming more like Christ. In Jesus mighty name, Amen.

SCRIPTURE READING

REFLECTION AND ENCOURAGEMENT

This verse reveals a beautiful progression of God's restorative work. When God moves, darkness does not linger; light breaks forth. Morning light speaks of clarity, new beginnings, and renewed hope. What felt hidden, delayed, or dim is suddenly illuminated by God's presence. God also promises that health shall spring forth speedily. This is not a slow recovery marked by fear or uncertainty; it is restoration energized by divine power. God's healing is purposeful and timely, reaching both body and soul. Righteousness going before you speaks of divine alignment and right standing. God prepares the way ahead of you, ordering your steps and removing obstacles before you arrive. And behind you, the glory of the Lord covers what is past, guarding you from attack and loss. You are surrounded, led, and protected. Isaiah 58:8 assures you that obedience and alignment with God usher in wholeness. Light replaces heaviness, health replaces weakness, and God's glory surrounds every step. You are not exposed; His care encompasses you.

MY LIGHT
BREAKS FORTH!

45

PRAYER AND DAILY DECLARATION

HEAVENLY Father, I thank You for Your promise of restoration, renewal, and divine intervention. You are the God who speaks light into darkness and brings clarity where there has been confusion. I receive Your light breaking into every hidden and heavy place of my life. Let hope rise like the morning sun. Let peace replace anxiety. Let clarity overcome uncertainty. Where there has been weakness, release strength. Where there has been a delay, release momentum. Let healing spring forth speedily in my body, in my mind, and in my spirit. Restore what has been drained. Renew what has been weary. Revive what has felt burdened. Let Your righteousness go before me, preparing my path and aligning my steps. Let Your glory surround me as protection and covering. May Your presence distinguish me and preserve me. I walk not in darkness, but in divine illumination. Today, I decree and declare God's light breaks forth in my life. Healing springs up speedily within me. Righteousness prepares my way. The glory of the Lord surrounds and covers me. Darkness has no authority over my path. I walk restored, protected, and renewed. I move forward in light, health, and divine covering, confident that the faithful hand of my God leads and sustains me. In Jesus mighty name, Amen.

SCRIPTURE READING

REFLECTION AND ENCOURAGEMENT

This verse reveals the heart of Jesus toward human weakness and need. Jesus makes it clear that He is not distant from pain or selective in compassion. He comes intentionally for those who recognize their need for healing. Sickness here is not limited to the physical; it includes emotional wounds, spiritual brokenness, and weary hearts. Jesus identifies Himself as the Physician. That means healing is not something you must earn or prove yourself worthy of. You do not have to be "whole" to come to Him. You come because you are not. Acknowledging need is not failure; it is the doorway to restoration. This passage also confronts the lie of self-sufficiency. Those who believe they are already whole often miss the healing available to them. But those who come honestly aware of their need receive care, attention, and restoration from Christ Himself. Let this verse encourage you: whatever feels broken, weak, or unresolved in your life is not something Jesus avoids. It is exactly where He meets you. He does not shame the sick. He heals them.

CHRIST IS MY HEALER!

PRAYER AND DAILY DECLARATION

HEAVENLY Father, I thank You for sending Jesus as the Great Physician, the One who heals not only the body, but the heart, the mind, and the soul. Thank You that I do not have to hide my weakness or pretend to be whole before coming to You. I come honestly and humbly, acknowledging every area where I need healing, restoration, and renewal. Lord, I trust both Your compassion and Your power. You are gentle with my wounds and mighty in Your ability to restore. Where I am weak, strengthen me with divine endurance. Where I am wounded, bring deep and lasting restoration. Where I am weary, breathe fresh life into my spirit. Touch every broken place, seen and unseen, and let Your healing virtue flow freely within me. Remove fear, shame, and hesitation from my heart. I receive Your healing with confidence, knowing that You meet me with mercy, not condemnation. Let Your peace settle over my thoughts and Your presence surround me with assurance. Today, I decree and declare Jesus is my Healer. I come to God without fear or pretense. Healing flows into every broken place. God's compassion surrounds and sustains me. Restoration is active and ongoing in my life. I rest in the care of Christ. I am being renewed from the inside out. The Physician of my soul is healing me completely and faithfully. In Jesus mighty name, Amen.

SCRIPTURE READING

REFLECTION AND ENCOURAGEMENT

This verse reveals the immeasurable power living within you as a believer. The same Spirit who raised Jesus from the dead now dwells in you, not as a distant influence, but as an active, life-giving presence. Resurrection power is not only a future hope; it is a present reality. To "quicken" means to make alive. God's Spirit brings vitality to what feels weak, worn, or lifeless. This includes physical strength, emotional resilience, spiritual passion, and renewed purpose. Where fatigue has lingered, God releases renewal. Where death seemed final, God releases life. Romans 8:11 assures you that God's power is not limited by your condition. The Spirit does not wait for ideal circumstances. He activates life right where you are. Your body, your mind, and your journey are all touched by the indwelling presence of God. This truth invites you to live with expectation. You are not sustained by willpower alone. You are energized by resurrection power. God's Spirit within you is continually working to restore, strengthen, and renew.

RESURRECTION POWER
LIVES IN ME!

PRAYER AND DAILY DECLARATION

HEAVENLY Father, I thank You for the gift of Your Holy Spirit dwelling within me. The same power that raised Jesus from the dead now lives and works in me. This is not distant power it is present, active, and life-giving. Thank You that I am not left to rely on my own strength but sustained by divine power from within. Let resurrection power renew my body, refresh my mind, and strengthen my spirit. Where I feel tired, breathe fresh life into me. Where weakness has tried to linger, release supernatural strength. Where discouragement has clouded my vision, awakened hope and renewed expectation. Quicken every area that feels stagnant. Revive every place that feels depleted. Lord, let Your Spirit energize my purpose and fortify my faith. I am not defined by limitation or exhaustion. I am empowered by the Spirit of the living God. Let divine vitality flow through my thoughts, my emotions, and my physical body. Establish me in strength that is not temporary but sustained by You. Today, I decree and declare The Spirit of God lives in me. Resurrection power is active within my body. Life overcomes weakness and weariness. I am strengthened from within by God's Spirit. Hope rises and faith is renewed. Divine vitality flows through me. I live energized, restored, and revived. I move forward alive, empowered, and sustained by the resurrection power of God dwelling within me. In Jesus mighty name, Amen.

SCRIPTURE READING

Mark 11:24 "Therefore I say unto you, What things soever ye desire, when ye pray, believe that ye receive them, and ye shall have them."

REFLECTION AND ENCOURAGEMENT

This verse reveals the powerful connection between prayer and faith. Jesus teaches that prayer is not merely about asking; it is about believing. Faith positions the heart to receive what prayer requests. To "believe that you receive" speaks of confidence in God's character, not uncertainty about His ability. It is trusting that God hears, responds, and acts according to His will. Faith-filled prayer operates from assurance rather than anxiety. It does not wait for visible evidence before trusting God's response. Instead, it rests in the certainty that God is faithful to His Word. When faith accompanies prayer, doubt loses its authority and expectation takes root. Believing prayer aligns your heart with heaven's timing and releases peace while you wait for manifestation. Jesus emphasizes that faith is active at the moment of prayer, not after the answer appears. This kind of faith does not deny reality; it submits reality to God's power. It allows you to pray boldly, trust fully, and walk forward confidently, knowing that God's promises are secure. Faith anchors your prayers in hope and steadies your heart through the waiting process. This verse encourages you to approach prayer with confidence, expectancy, and trust. When you pray believing, your heart remains settled, your faith is strengthened, and your posture becomes one of surrender rather than striving. God honors faith that trusts Him completely and rests in His faithfulness.

CONFIDENT IN PRAYER!

PRAYER AND DAILY DECLARATION

HEAVENLY Father, I thank You for the gift of faith and for the assurance that You hear me when I pray. You are attentive to my voice, and Your promises are secure. I come before You with confidence not because of my own merit, but because of Your faithfulness. I trust Your Word and rest in the certainty that You respond according to Your perfect will. Strengthen my heart to pray with boldness and expectation. Remove hesitation, fear, and doubt from my spirit. Teach me to believe at the moment I pray, anchoring my trust in who You are rather than in what I see. Align my desires with heaven's purpose so that my prayers reflect Your truth and Your timing. Today, I decree and declare I pray with faith and confidence. My heart is aligned with heaven. When I pray, I believe, and I receive by faith. Doubt has no authority over my spirit. God's promises are secure and unshakable. My prayers are effective because they are rooted in faith. My faith is active and unwavering. My heart remains steady while I await manifestation. I walk in peace, confidence, and assurance, knowing that what God has spoken, He will faithfully bring to pass. In Jesus mighty name, Amen.

SCRIPTURE READING

Jeremiah 33:3 "Call unto me, and I will answer thee, and shew thee great and mighty things, which thou knowest not."

REFLECTION AND ENCOURAGEMENT

This scripture is a powerful invitation into divine intimacy and revelation. God does not merely tolerate your questions; He invites them. "Call unto Me" speaks of relationship an open line of communication between God and His people. Prayer is not a last resort; it is an access point to heaven's wisdom. God promises not only to answer but to reveal. His response goes beyond surface understanding into "great and mighty things" truths that are hidden, inaccessible by human reasoning, and beyond natural knowledge. This verse reminds you that there are dimensions of God's plan that cannot be discovered through effort alone. Revelation flows from connection. When you call on God with sincerity and trust, He unveils insight, direction, and clarity that could not be reached by intellect, experience, or strategy. What feels unknown, confusing, or locked away is not withheld to frustrate you; it is reserved to be revealed through communion with Him. God's desire is not secrecy but stewardship. He reveals mysteries to guide, prepare, and align you with His purpose. As you lean into prayer, He opens your understanding, sharpens your discernment, and brings light to areas that once felt closed. This promise assures you that you are not walking blindly. Heaven responds when you call. Answers are released, and divine insight is made available to those who seek Him. Your future is not hidden from God, and what He reveals will equip you to walk forward with confidence, wisdom, and peace.

GREAT AND MIGHTY THINGS AWAIT!

PRAYER AND DAILY DECLARATION

HEAVENLY Father, I thank You for inviting me into relationship and revelation. Thank You for the assurance that when I call upon You, You hear me and respond with wisdom, clarity, and divine insight. You are attentive to my voice, and Your promises are faithful and secure. I come before You with confidence, not because I understand everything, but because You do. I trust Your Word and rest in the certainty that You reveal what I need according to Your perfect will. Strengthen my heart to seek You with expectation. Remove hesitation, distraction, and doubt from my spirit. Teach me to call upon You with confidence, believing that You answer and unveil great and mighty things. Align my heart with heaven's perspective so that I am prepared to receive the insight, direction, and revelation You release. Today, I decree and declare that I call upon the Lord, and He answers me. My heart is aligned with heaven's wisdom. Divine revelation flows into my life. Hidden things are made clear. Confusion is replaced with understanding. My spiritual discernment is sharpened. My faith is active and receptive. My heart remains steady as I await full manifestation. I walk in clarity, confidence, and peace, knowing that the God who invites me to call upon Him faithfully reveals great and mighty things in His perfect time. In Jesus mighty name, Amen.

SCRIPTURE READING

Jeremiah 29:11–12 For I know the thoughts that I think toward you, saith the LORD, thoughts of peace, and not of evil, to give you an expected end. Then shall ye call upon me, and ye shall go and pray unto me, and I will hearken unto you.

REFLECTION AND ENCOURAGEMENT

This passage is a profound reminder that delay does not mean denial. God speaks these words to His people while they are still in captivity, not after their deliverance. This alone reveals something powerful: God's promises are not dependent on your current condition. Even in restricted seasons, His plan is already unfolding. The waiting period was long, seventy years, but it was not empty. God was not absent, distracted, or indifferent. He was working according to a divine timetable that would lead to restoration, peace, and fulfillment. What felt like a delay was divine preparation. God reassures His people by revealing His heart: "I know the thoughts that I think toward you." His plans are intentional, thoughtful, and rooted in peace. Even when circumstances feel harsh or confusing, His intentions toward you remain good. Waiting seasons are not wasted seasons; they are formative seasons where faith is strengthened, character is refined, and dependence on God is deepened. This passage also reveals that restoration is connected to a relationship. God invites His people to call, pray, seek, and pursue Him wholeheartedly. Delay becomes a doorway to deeper intimacy. When you seek Him with your whole heart, He promises to be found. God is not distant in delay. He is deeply present, drawing you closer and aligning your heart with His promises. Captivity, whether emotional, spiritual, financial, or situational, is never permanent when God declares restoration. He gathers, restores, and repositions His people. What feels like exile today will become a testimony tomorrow. God's timing is precise, His promises are sure, and your expected end remains intact.

GOD IS DOING

A NEW THING

PRAYER AND DAILY DECLARATION

HEAVENLY Father, I thank You for Your faithfulness and for the assurance that You are intentional with every season of my life. Nothing about my journey is wasted or overlooked. Even when I do not fully understand the timing or the process, I trust that You are working all things together for my good and for Your glory. You are not idle in my waiting; You are active in my becoming. Lord, as You do a new thing in me, renew my mind, refine my character, and align my desires with Your will. Break every pattern that no longer serves Your purpose. Remove every limitation, fear, or mindset that resists growth. Let transformation begin within my heart and flow into every area of my life. Today, I decree and declare that the Lord is mindful of me. His thoughts toward me are thoughts of peace and not of evil. My waiting season is purposeful and productive. When I call upon the Lord, He hears and responds. As I seek Him wholeheartedly, I will find Him. Every form of captivity, limitation, and restriction is broken. Divine restoration and alignment are unfolding in my life. The manifestation of my expected end is secured by God's promise. I surrender my timeline to You and trust Your divine process. I rest in the assurance that what You have spoken, You will surely perform. I step forward renewed, aligned, and confident that You are doing a new thing in me and through me. In Jesus mighty name, Amen.

SCRIPTURE READING

Deuteronomy 30:19 "I call heaven and earth to record this day against you, that I have set before you life and death, blessing and cursing: therefore choose life, that both thou and thy seed may live."

REFLECTION AND ENCOURAGEMENT

This verse stands as one of the most powerful invitations God gives to humanity, the gift and responsibility of choice. God does not coerce obedience or force blessing. Instead, He lovingly presents the options and then urges us toward what leads to life. By calling heaven and earth as witnesses, God underscores the gravity and eternal significance of every decision we make. Choosing life goes beyond physical existence. It is a deliberate alignment with God's will, truth, and promises. Each choice rooted in obedience, faith, and wisdom releases consequences that stretch far beyond the present moment. What you choose today does not end with you; it becomes a legacy that touches generations yet to come. God's heart is unmistakably clear: He desires life, blessing, and continuity for you and your descendants. Even when circumstances appear restrictive or the cost of obedience feels heavy, God reminds you that life remains accessible through repentance, faith, trust, and surrender. Choosing life often requires courage, discipline, and humility, but it always leads to peace and purpose. This verse reassures you that blessings have already been placed within reach. You are not powerless, overlooked, or trapped by circumstance. With God's guidance, you can choose what nurtures life, protects peace, and establishes lasting impact. Every God-honoring decision becomes a seed planted today, harvested tomorrow, and remembered by generations.

CHOOSING GOD IS CHOOSING LIFE!

PRAYER AND DAILY DECLARATION

HEAVENLY Father, I thank You for setting before me the path of life and blessing. You do not leave me without direction; You lovingly guide my steps and reveal the way that leads to wholeness, peace, and purpose. Thank You for caring not only about my present, but about the generations connected to me. My choices matter, and You give me wisdom to choose well. Teach me to recognize that choosing You is choosing life. In every decision great or small help me align with Your truth and not my emotions. Guard me from impulsive choices and from paths that appear good but do not lead to Your will. Strengthen me to walk in obedience, even when it requires courage and discipline. Let blessing flow through my surrender. Let wisdom govern my decisions. May my obedience release life not only in me, but in my household and future generations. Establish my steps in righteousness and anchor my heart in faithfulness. Today, I decree and declare I choose life in every decision I make. I align my choices with God's truth and wisdom. Blessing flows through my obedience. My decisions bring life to my household and generations after me. I walk intentionally and confidently in God's will. Father, give me discernment to choose wisely, courage to choose boldly, and grace to live faithfully. Let my life testify that choosing You always leads to life, peace, and lasting fruit. In Jesus mighty name, Amen.

SCRIPTURE READING

1 Peter 2:9 "But ye are a chosen generation, a royal priesthood, an holy nation, a peculiar people; that ye should shew forth the praises of him who hath called you out of darkness into his marvelous light."

REFLECTION AND ENCOURAGEMENT

This verse is a powerful declaration of identity. Before it speaks about what you do, it reminds you of who you are. You are chosen. Your life is not accidental, overlooked, or insignificant. God intentionally selected you and set you apart with purpose. Apostle Peter describes believers as a royal priesthood and a holy nation. Royalty speaks of authority and dignity; priesthood speaks of access and responsibility. You are not distant from God you have direct access to Him. You are called to carry His presence, reflect His character, and represent His truth in the earth. Holiness here does not mean perfection; it means being set apart for divine purpose. The phrase "peculiar people" speaks of distinction. You are not meant to blend into darkness or conform to every surrounding influence. Your life carries a different standard because it carries a different light. God has called you out of darkness out of confusion, shame, and spiritual blindness and brought you into His marvelous light. That light brings clarity, direction, and identity. This verse also reveals purpose: that you should show forth His praises. Your life is meant to reflect gratitude, testimony, and visible transformation. When others see your peace in difficulty, your integrity in pressure, and your hope in uncertainty, they see evidence of the One who called you. Let this encourage you today: you are chosen, positioned, and purposed. You are not defined by your past, your mistakes, or others' opinions. You belong to God, and your life carries divine significance. Walk confidently in that identity. You have been called out and you now walk in marvelous light.

CHOSEN AND SET APART!

PRAYER AND DAILY DECLARATION

HEAVENLY Father, I thank You that I am chosen by You. My life is not random, forgotten, or overlooked. You have called me out of darkness and into Your marvelous light. Thank You for giving me a new identity not defined by my past, my failures, or the opinions of others but defined by Your truth and Your grace. Teach me to walk confidently in who You say I am. Remind me that I am part of a royal priesthood, with access to Your presence and authority through Christ. Let my life reflect dignity, integrity, and holiness. Set my heart apart for Your purposes and align my desires with Your will. Help me to show forth Your praises in the way I live. Let my words carry light. Let my decisions reflect wisdom. Let my responses demonstrate love. May my life testify that I belong to You and that Your light transforms everything it touches. Today, I decree and declare I am chosen by God. I am part of a royal priesthood. I am set apart for divine purpose. Darkness no longer defines me. I walk in God's marvelous light. My identity is secure in Christ. My life reflects His glory. I carry His presence with confidence and humility. I walk boldly as one called, redeemed, and positioned to shine. In Jesus mighty name, Amen.

SCRIPTURE READING

Philippians 4:13 "I can do all things through Christ, which strengtheneth me."

REFLECTION AND ENCOURAGEMENT

This scripture is a powerful declaration of where true strength is found. It reminds you that your ability to endure, overcome, and succeed does not originate from your own capacity, experience, or resources, but it flows directly from Christ. When your strength feels insufficient, Christ becomes more than enough. Life will present moments that stretch you beyond what feels comfortable or manageable. There will be seasons when responsibility feels heavy, challenges seem unending, and confidence begins to waver. In those moments, this verse anchors your heart in an unchanging truth: Christ supplies strength that does not run out. His strength is not emotional, circumstantial, or temporary; it is constant and sustaining. Apostle Paul's declaration was born from experience, not ease. He learned that Christ's strength is present in every condition, whether in abundance or lack, certainty or uncertainty. This means your current season does not disqualify you. Instead, it becomes the very place where Christ's power is revealed most clearly through you. Through Christ, you are not merely surviving; you are equipped to rise, endure, and move forward with purpose. His strength enables you to push past fear, remain steady under pressure, and walk boldly in obedience to God's call. Nothing assigned to you is too great when Christ is the source sustaining you. What feels impossible in your own power becomes achievable when you rely fully on Him.

MY PORTION IS ASSIGNED BY GOD!

PRAYER AND DAILY DECLARATION

HEAVENLY Father, I thank You that my strength comes from Christ and not from myself. I acknowledge that apart from You, I can do nothing of eternal value, but through Christ, I am fully equipped, sustained, and empowered for every assignment You have placed before me. I refuse to rely on limited human ability when divine strength is available to me. When I feel inadequate, remind me that Your grace is sufficient. When I feel stretched beyond capacity, remind me that Your power is made perfect in weakness. Teach me to lean into Your strength instead of striving in my own. Let dependence become my confidence, and surrender become my stability. Today, I decree and declare that Christ strengthens me in all that I do. I am not limited by fear, weakness, or doubt. Through Christ, I receive grace, wisdom, endurance, and clarity. Every assignment before me is achievable through His strength. I walk in confidence, faith, and divine empowerment. I do not shrink back from responsibility. I do not collapse under pressure. I rise in the strength that Christ supplies. Lord, I rely on Your strength daily. Sustain me when I feel weary. Guide me when I feel uncertain. Stabilize me when challenges arise. Let Your strength flow through my mind, my words, my work, and my decisions. I step forward assured, capable, and bold, not because of who I am alone, but because of who You are in me. In Jesus mighty name, Amen.

SCRIPTURE READING

Psalm 27:1 "The LORD is my light and my salvation; whom shall I fear? The LORD is the strength of my life; of whom shall I be afraid?"

REFLECTION AND ENCOURAGEMENT

This verse is a bold proclamation of fearless confidence rooted in God's presence. It reminds you that when the Lord is your light, darkness, whether fear, confusion, or uncertainty, has no authority over your life. God does not merely point the way forward; He becomes the illumination that guides every step you take. To declare that the Lord is your salvation is to affirm that deliverance is not dependent on circumstances, timing, or human intervention. Salvation speaks of rescue, safety, and preservation. When God stands as your deliverer, fear loses its power to intimidate or control your heart. You are not vulnerable to what surrounds you because you are secured by who surrounds you. God is not simply a source of strength; you are not required to summon courage on your own. He becomes the very strength of your life, sustaining you when you feel weak, steadying you when you feel shaken, and empowering you when the road ahead feels uncertain. His strength does not fluctuate with seasons or situations; it remains constant, faithful, and dependable. This scripture reassures you that no challenge, opposition, or unknown future can stand against the presence of the Lord. When God surrounds you, courage replaces fear, peace replaces anxiety, and confidence replaces doubt. You are empowered to move forward boldly, knowing that the One who guards your life never fails and never leaves.

MATURITY IS FORMING IN ME!

PRAYER AND DAILY DECLARATION

HEAVENLY Father, I thank You that You are my light, my salvation, and the strength of my life. Because You are with me, I do not have to remain spiritually immature or ruled by fear. Your presence dispels darkness and steadily forms courage within me. As I walk with You, You are shaping my character, stabilizing my faith, and strengthening my inner man. Lord, let spiritual maturity take root in my heart. Where fear once controlled my reactions, establish confidence. Where anxiety once shaped my thinking, anchor me in peace. Teach me to respond with wisdom instead of impulse, faith instead of doubt, and steadiness instead of instability. Form in me a courageous spirit that trusts You even when circumstances feel uncertain. As You grow me, refine my thoughts, purify my motives, and align my responses with Your truth. Let my maturity be evident in how I speak, decide, forgive, and persevere. Strengthen me to stand firm under pressure and to walk consistently in the light You provide. Today, I decree and declare that the Lord is my light and my salvation. Fear has no authority over my life. The Lord is the strength of my life. Spiritual maturity is forming within me. My faith is stable and growing. I respond with wisdom, courage, and peace. God's presence surrounds, sustains, and protects me. I am developing strength of character and depth of faith. I move forward steady, confident, and grounded in truth. I trust You completely, knowing that as I walk with You, I am being strengthened, refined, and established in lasting maturity. In Jesus mighty name, Amen.

SCRIPTURE READING

REFLECTION AND ENCOURAGEMENT

This verse is a strong declaration that God's promises are not theoretical; they are meant to be walked into and possessed. God speaks in the past tense: "I have given unto you." Before Joshua ever moved, the territory was already assigned. This reminds you that God prepares provision, opportunity, and victory ahead of your obedience. Possession follows movement. God does not ask you to understand every detail before stepping forward; He asks you to trust Him enough to move. Faith becomes active when you place your feet where God has spoken. Each step taken in obedience activates what God has already released in the spirit. This passage also teaches that fear and hesitation are the greatest enemies of possession. The land was promised, but it still required movement. God honors forward motion steps taken with faith, even when confidence feels small. As you move, clarity increases, courage strengthens, and authority is established. You are not trespassing into unfamiliar territory; you are walking into a promise. What lies before you is not random or uncertain; it has already been secured by God's word. Your steps matter. Where you tread in faith, God establishes ownership, influence, and fulfillment.

STEP INTO THE PROMISE!

PRAYER AND DAILY DECLARATION

HEAVENLY Father, I thank You for the promises You have spoken over my life. Your Word is faithful, and Your covenant is secure. What You have declared will not return void. I trust that You go before me, preparing the way, aligning circumstances, and establishing my steps according to Your divine plan. Lord, give me the courage to move forward in obedience and confidence. Where hesitation tries to delay me, release bold faith. Where fear attempts to intimidate me strengthen my resolve. Teach me that promise requires participation, that faith must move, trust must step, and obedience must act. I refuse to remain where You have called me to advance. Today, I decree and declare that every step I take is ordered by the Lord. I possess what God has promised me. Forward movement unlocks my divine inheritance. Fear and hesitation have no authority over my decisions. My path is secured and established by God's Word. Doors open as I walk in obedience. Provision meets me as I step in faith. Grace accompanies every assignment attached to my name. I move forward with clarity, boldness, and expectation, knowing that what You have promised is not distant, it is prepared for me to possess. I step boldly into purpose, alignment, and fulfillment, confident that the God who promised is faithful to perform. In Jesus mighty name, Amen.

SCRIPTURE READING

Isaiah 54:15–17 "No weapon that is formed against thee shall prosper; and every tongue that shall rise against thee in judgment thou shalt condemn…"

REFLECTION AND ENCOURAGEMENT

This passage is a powerful assurance that God Himself stands as your defender. It acknowledges that opposition may arise, plans may form, and words may be spoken, but it clearly declares that none of these things has authority to prevail over what God has established in your life. God makes it clear that not every gathering or attack has His approval. What is formed without His authority cannot endure. Even when weapons are crafted or accusations are raised, God renders them ineffective. Their presence does not equal their success. This promise is rooted not in human effort, but in divine covenant. Your righteousness comes from the Lord, not from self-defense or explanation. Because God justifies you, you do not need to fight every battle. He fights on your behalf. This passage invites you to live with confidence rather than fear. You are not surrounded by threats; your life is surrounded by God's power. What was meant to harm you will be silenced, and what rose against you will fall away. Your victory is not something you must chase; it is your heritage.

THIS IS YOUR HERITAGE
STAND SECURE!

PRAYER AND DAILY DECLARATION

HEAVENLY Father, I thank You for being my defender, my protector, and my righteous Judge. You see every plan formed, every word spoken, and every attempt made against my life. Nothing escapes Your awareness, and nothing rises above Your authority. You are sovereign over every circumstance, and I rest in the assurance that my life is guarded by Your covenant. Lord, I release the burden of self-defense. I lay down the need to justify myself or fight battles in my own strength. Where accusations have tried to rise, I receive Your justification. Where opposition has tried to intimidate me, I receive Your peace and steady assurance. You are my advocate, and You uphold my cause with righteousness and truth. Today, I decree and declare that no weapon formed against me shall prosper. Every false word spoken against me is silenced. God Himself defends my cause. Victory belongs to me as a servant of the Lord. Divine assurance steadies my heart. This is my heritage. I stand secure, confident, and unshaken. I walk forward without fear, knowing that the Lord surrounds me, strengthens me, and establishes me in victory. My life is protected, preserved, and positioned by the faithful hand of my God. In Jesus mighty name, Amen.

SCRIPTURE READING

Psalm 34:7 "The angel of the LORD encampeth round about them that fear him, and delivereth them."

REFLECTION AND ENCOURAGEMENT

This verse is a powerful reassurance that God's protection over your life is active, intentional, and deeply personal. It reveals that divine security is not merely a comforting thought; it is a present spiritual reality. To "encamp" means to set up a guarded position, like an army stationed around you. God assigns angelic protection to surround His people. When you fear the Lord, walking in reverence, faith, and obedience, you are never exposed or unguarded. Heaven is actively involved in your safety. Even when you cannot see what is happening in the unseen realm, God has already positioned protection around you. His watch over your life is constant and deliberate. This scripture also speaks of deliverance. God not only surrounds you; He rescues you. There are dangers you will never know you avoided, traps that never formed fully, and attacks that were stopped before they reached you. God intervenes quietly yet powerfully, removing you from harm and shielding you from fear, confusion, and destruction. When uncertainty arises, this verse reminds you that you are not alone in the battle. You are not navigating life unprotected. God's protection is not delayed, and His deliverance is not occasional. The angel of the Lord remains on guard, and the Lord Himself ensures that you are kept, covered, and brought safely through every situation.

REJOICING REPLACES FEAR!

PRAYER AND DAILY DECLARATION

HEAVENLY Father, I thank You for Your constant protection and for assigning heaven's help over my life. You are not distant or unaware; You are actively watching, guarding, and delivering me even from dangers I cannot see. Thank You that Your protection is intentional and Your care is personal. When fear tries to rise, remind me that I am surrounded. When uncertainty whispers, anchor my heart in the truth that heaven stands guard over me. Let rejoicing replace fear. Let gratitude silence anxiety. Let confidence grow where intimidation once attempted to take root. I trust that You are delivering me from seen and unseen threats. You are shielding my mind from torment, my heart from panic, and my path from destruction. My safety is not accidental; it is divinely secure. I do not walk alone, and I do not walk unprotected. Today, I decree and declare that the angel of the Lord encamps around me. I am divinely protected on every side. Fear has no authority over my life. I am delivered from harm and hidden threats. No plan of darkness can prevail against me. My home is covered. My steps are ordered. My future is secured by God. I choose rejoicing over fear. I walk forward in peace and assurance, confident that heaven surrounds me and the Lord Himself is my refuge, my shield, and my deliverer. In Jesus mighty name, Amen.

SCRIPTURE READING

2 Corinthians 4:17 "For our light affliction, which is but for a moment, worketh for us a far more exceeding and eternal weight of glory."

REFLECTION AND ENCOURAGEMENT

This verse shifts your perspective from temporary pressure to eternal purpose. What feels heavy now is described as "light" when compared to the glory that is coming. God does not dismiss your affliction, but He reframes it. Trials are not permanent fixtures; they are momentary processes producing something far greater than what you can currently see. Affliction is not meaningless. It is productive. It is shaping endurance, strengthening character, and deepening your dependence on God. What feels like pressure is actually preparation. What feels like delay is developing eternal perspective. God is not allowing hardship without intention; He is working through it. The phrase "weight of glory" speaks of substance, permanence, and eternal reward. While suffering may feel intense in the present, it does not compare to the lasting glory being formed through it. Your trials are not the final chapter. They are the refining ground for something eternal. This passage reminds you that present discomfort cannot outweigh future promise. The hardship may be visible, but the glory is certain. God is building something within you that time cannot erase and circumstances cannot destroy.

PRESENT SUFFERING PRODUCES ETERNAL GLORY!

PRAYER AND DAILY DECLARATION

HEAVENLY Father, I thank You that my present afflictions are not wasted in Your hands. Even when the weight feels heavy, I trust that You are producing something eternal within me. Strengthen my heart to endure with faith, patience, and steady hope. Guard my mind from discouragement and my spirit from despair. Form perseverance within me and refine my character through this season. Let every trial deepen my dependence on You and increase my spiritual maturity. Today, I decree and declare with confidence that every challenge I face is working for my good and for God's glory. My present affliction is light compared to the eternal weight of glory You are preparing. I will not lose heart. I will not grow weary. God is strengthening my faith, shaping my endurance, and expanding my capacity. I fix my eyes not on what is seen, but on what is eternal. My hope is anchored beyond circumstance. I walk forward with confidence, knowing glory outweighs every trial. In Jesus mighty name. Amen.

SCRIPTURE READING

Isaiah 40:31 "But they that wait upon the LORD shall renew their strength; they shall mount up with wings as eagles; they shall run, and not be weary; and they shall walk, and not faint."

REFLECTION AND ENCOURAGEMENT

This verse is a powerful promise for seasons when strength feels depleted and endurance feels tested. God does not ask you to rely on your own capacity. He invites you to wait on Him. Waiting on the Lord is not passive; it is a posture of trust, expectation, and dependence. Renewal is God's response to waiting. When you pause in His presence, He exchanges your weariness for His strength. What feels drained is replenished. What feels heavy is lifted. God restores you from the inside out, giving you the ability to rise above limitations and discouragement. Mounting up with wings like eagles speaks of perspective and elevation. God lifts you above what once overwhelmed you. Running without weariness and walking without fainting reveal sustained strength not just for sudden breakthroughs, but for everyday faithfulness. This passage reassures you that endurance is grace-powered. God sustains you for both the journey and the destination. As you wait on Him, He renews your strength again and again.

STRENGTH RENEWED

IN GOD'S PRESENCE!

PRAYER AND DAILY DECLARATION

HEAVENLY Father, I thank You that You are the source of my strength and the restorer of my soul. When I grow weary or burdened, You do not leave me depleted. As I wait on You, You renew me from the inside out. In Your presence, heaviness lifts, clarity returns, and strength is restored. Today, I release every burden, every pressure, and every weight I was never meant to carry alone. I exchange exhaustion for endurance and anxiety for peace. Teach me to wait with trust, not frustration with expectation, not doubt. As I remain in Your presence, infuse my heart with courage and my spirit with resilience. Today, I decree and declare that the Lord renews my strength. I rise above weariness and discouragement. I run my race with endurance and do not faint. God sustains me in every season. Renewal and perseverance are my portion. I wait on You with faith and confidence. You lift me when I feel weak. You strengthen me when I feel overwhelmed. You carry me forward by Your sustaining grace. I receive renewed strength for today and for the journey ahead, confident that Your presence is my refuge and my constant source of power. In Jesus mighty name, Amen.

SCRIPTURE READING

Psalm 46:1 "God is our refuge and strength, a very present help in trouble."

REFLECTION AND ENCOURAGEMENT

This verse offers deep reassurance for every season of uncertainty, pressure, or distress. God is not distant when trouble arises. He is very present. His help is not delayed, conditional, or uncertain. It is immediate, intentional, and reliable. To call God a refuge means He is a safe place you can run to without fear. A refuge is not merely protection from danger; it is shelter, rest, and security. When life feels overwhelming, God does not stand on the sidelines. He becomes your hiding place. God is also described as strong. This means He does not only shield you from difficulty; He empowers you to endure it. When your strength feels depleted, His strength becomes available. You are not expected to carry the weight alone. God supplies what you lack. This passage reminds you that trouble does not signal abandonment. It often becomes the place where God's nearness is most clearly revealed. You are not unsupported, unseen, or forgotten. God is present, powerful, and actively involved in helping you through.

A VERY PRESENT HELP!

PRAYER AND DAILY DECLARATION

HEAVENLY Father, I thank You for being my refuge and my strength. In every season whether calm or uncertain You remain my safe place. You are not distant in times of trouble; You are present, attentive, and actively working on my behalf. When circumstances feel heavy and answers seem unclear, remind me that I can run to You without hesitation or fear. Lord, when my own strength feels depleted, teach me to rely fully on Yours. Help me to stop striving in my own ability and instead rest in Your sustaining presence. Where anxiety tries to rise, anchor me in trust. Where pressure tries to overwhelm me, steady my heart with Your peace. Today, I decree and declare that God is my refuge and my secure dwelling place. His strength upholds and sustains me. Divine help is present in my situation. I am not overwhelmed, and I am not abandoned. I am supported by God's unfailing care. Every burden I carry, I place into Your hands. Every concern, I surrender to Your wisdom. Every challenge, I entrust to Your power. I trust You to sustain me, strengthen me, and guide me forward with clarity and confidence. I move ahead in peace, knowing that the God who shelters me is the God who carries me through. In Jesus mighty name, Amen.

SCRIPTURE READING

REFLECTION AND ENCOURAGEMENT

This verse speaks directly to seasons of weariness. It acknowledges moments when strength feels low and perseverance feels difficult. God does not overlook fatigue. He addresses it with compassion, encouragement, and renewal. To "lift up the hands" speaks of renewed posture returning to worship, readiness, and hope. To "strengthen the feeble knees" speaks of restored stability and endurance. God understands when the journey has been long, but He reminds you that weariness is not your destination; it is a moment, not a conclusion. Hebrews 12:12 is not a demand to pretend you are strong. It is an invitation to receive strength. God supplies what you lack. When your resolve feels thin and your steps feel heavy, He reinforces you from within and steadies you to continue forward. This verse reassures you that discouragement does not disqualify you, and fatigue does not cancel purpose. God is not rushing you. He is strengthening you. You are being renewed for continuation, sustained not by willpower, but by grace.

STRENGTH FOR THE JOURNEY!

PRAYER AND DAILY DECLARATION

HEAVENLY Father, I thank You that You see my weariness and respond with compassion and strength. You are attentive to every burden I carry and every step I take. When my energy feels depleted and my resolve feels stretched, You meet me with sustaining grace. You do not ask me to continue in my own power; You supply what I lack. Where I feel tired, renew me from within. Where discouragement has tried to settle, awaken hope again. Where my resolve feels weak, steady me with Your peace and assurance. Teach me that the journey is not walked alone. Your presence walks with me, strengthening my hands and stabilizing my steps. Today, I choose to rise again not by striving, but by trusting. I receive fresh strength for the path ahead. Strengthen my heart to endure, my mind to remain focused, and my spirit to persevere. Today, I decree and declare that my strength is renewed by God. Weariness does not define me. My steps are steady and supported. Perseverance rises within me. God empowers me to continue. I am not exhausted beyond recovery. I am not defeated by delay. I am sustained by divine grace. I move forward restored, supported, and confident, knowing that the God who called me is the God who strengthens me for every mile of the journey. In Jesus mighty name, Amen.

SCRIPTURE READING

Psalm 18:29 "For by thee I have run through a troop; and by my God have I leaped over a wall."

REFLECTION AND ENCOURAGEMENT

This verse is a triumphant declaration of what is possible when God becomes the source of your strength. David is not boasting in personal ability; he is testifying to divine enablement. What would normally require force, strategy, or prolonged struggle is overcome through God's power alone. To run through a troop speaks of confronting opposition head-on and emerging victorious. It represents moments when resistance rises, pressure increases, and obstacles appear determined to stop your progress. Yet with God, opposition does not overpower you; it is overcome. Strength flows not from fearlessness, but from confidence in God's presence and power. To leap over a wall speaks of supernatural elevation. Walls are barriers, limitations, delays, systems, or fears that appear immovable. But God does not always remove the wall; sometimes He empowers you to rise above it. What once blocked your path becomes a testimony of a breakthrough. This verse reminds you that advancement in God is not passive. Faith moves forward with courage, trusting God to supply strength beyond natural limits. Breakthrough is released when you rely on God rather than retreat from resistance. With Him, momentum replaces stagnation, courage replaces hesitation, and victory replaces defeat. So be encouraged, what stands before you is not greater than the God who strengthens you. You are not called to survive opposition, but to overcome it. By God, you move forward. By God, you rise higher. By God, you win.

LEAPING OVER WALLS!

PRAYER AND DAILY DECLARATION

HEAVENLY Father, I thank You for being my strength in every battle and my power in every moment of resistance. You are the One who equips my hands, steadies my feet, and fortifies my spirit. When obstacles rise and barriers appear immovable, I remember that You are greater than every wall before me. Without You I cannot overcome, but with You nothing can stand against what You have ordained for my life. Lord, strengthen me for breakthrough. Where resistance has slowed me, release fresh momentum. Where limitations once defined my progress, establish divine expansion. Remind me that barriers are not final they are opportunities for Your power to be revealed. Give me courage to advance, faith to press forward, and endurance to refuse retreat. Today, I decree and declare that God strengthens me for breakthrough. Every barrier before me is overcome by His power. I leap over every wall that once limited my progress. No opposition can cancel God's purpose for my life. My victory is secured by God's strength, not my own. I move forward with courage and confidence. Momentum replaces stagnation. Divine acceleration propels me into promises. What once stood in my way will now testify to the power of God at work within me. I rise above resistance, strengthened by grace and empowered by faith. In Jesus mighty name, Amen.

SCRIPTURE READING

Lamentations 3:22–23 "It is of the LORD'S mercies that we are not consumed, because his compassions fail not. They are new every morning: great is thy faithfulness."

REFLECTION AND ENCOURAGEMENT

These verses gently yet powerfully remind us that our lives are sustained not by our strength, perfection, or consistency but by God's mercy. Every breath you take and every new day you see is evidence that God's compassion is actively at work in your life. Even in difficult seasons, His mercy stands as the reason you are still standing. God's mercy is not exhausted by yesterday's failures or overwhelmed by today's challenges. It is continual, intentional, and sufficient. Each morning, God releases fresh compassion tailored for the day ahead. You are not living off leftovers from the past; you are receiving new grace designed for your present moment. This passage also highlights God's unwavering faithfulness. Circumstances may change, emotions may rise and fall, and seasons may shift, but God remains steady. His faithfulness is the anchor that holds you when life feels uncertain. Even when your strength feels limited, His faithfulness carries you forward. These verses invite you to embrace new beginnings with confidence. Yesterday does not have authority over today. God does not recycle mercy. He renews it. Each sunrise is an invitation to start again, walk forward in hope, and trust that your future is upheld by His unfailing love.

NEW MERCIES DAILY!

PRAYER AND DAILY DECLARATION

HEAVENLY Father, I thank You for Your mercy that sustains my life and Your faithfulness that never fails. Your compassion is not occasional it is constant. Each morning, You meet me with grace that is new, strength that is sufficient, and love that is unwavering. I receive this day as a fresh beginning, covered by Your mercy and anchored in Your goodness. Thank You that I do not walk alone into today. Your mercy walks beside me, correcting me when I falter, lifting me when I stumble, and preserving me when I feel vulnerable. Where I have fallen short, Your mercy restores me. Where I have felt discouraged, Your faithfulness steadies me. Yesterday does not define my future, and past mistakes do not cancel Your purpose over my life. Today, I decree and declare that God's mercy preserves and protects me. His compassion is new to me this morning. God's faithfulness upholds every area of my life. My past does not determine my future. Grace empowers me to begin again. I walk forward in renewed hope, strengthened by mercy and sustained by faithfulness. My heart is steady. My spirit is encouraged. My steps are guided by divine grace. I embrace this new day with gratitude and confidence, knowing that Your mercy walks with me and Your faithfulness carries me into all You have prepared. In Jesus mighty name, Amen.

SCRIPTURE READING

REFLECTION AND ENCOURAGEMENT

This passage gently redirects your focus from uncertainty to assurance. It acknowledges the instinct to look around for help toward people, systems, or visible solutions, yet it firmly anchors your confidence in the Lord, the Maker of heaven and earth. Your help does not come from limited sources; it comes from the unlimited power of God Himself. When pressure increases and strength feels insufficient, this verse reminds you that you are not meant to carry life alone. God positions Himself as your helper, present, attentive, and capable. He is not distant or overwhelmed by your need. The same God who formed creation sustains you with precision and care. Lifting your eyes is an act of faith. It is choosing trust over fear and dependence over self-reliance. As you look to the Lord, He supplies what is needed for the moment: strength for today, wisdom for decisions, peace for the heart, and endurance for the journey ahead. This reflection assures you that divine support is constant. God's help does not waver with circumstances or emotions. He stands ready, strengthening you from within and surrounding you with His faithful presence. You are supported, upheld, and never abandoned.

MY HELP COMES FROM THE LORD!

PRAYER AND DAILY DECLARATION

HEAVENLY Father, I lift my eyes to You, acknowledging that You alone are my true source of help, strength, and unfailing support. When circumstances shift, and my own ability feels insufficient, I remember that my help does not come from people, positions, or resources; it comes from You, the Maker of heaven and earth. You are sovereign, capable, and attentive to my every need. Lord, teach me to look upward before I look around. When pressure increases and uncertainty rises, anchor my heart in the assurance that You are near. You sustain me in every season in abundance and in lack, in clarity and in confusion. You are not limited by what limits me. You are not shaken by what unsettles me. Today, I decree and declare that My help comes from the Lord. I am supported and strengthened by God. I am not overwhelmed, for the Lord upholds me. Divine strength renews me daily. God's power sustains my spirit. I am not alone in my challenges. I am not unsupported in my assignments. I am upheld by the faithful hand of my God. I walk forward with confidence, knowing that heaven is actively involved in my life. I rest in Your presence, draw strength from Your power, and move ahead with peace, fully assured that You are with me and You are for me. In Jesus mighty name, Amen

SCRIPTURE READING

Psalm 125:2 "As the mountains are round about Jerusalem, so the LORD is round about his people from henceforth even for ever."

REFLECTION AND ENCOURAGEMENT

This verse paints a powerful and deeply reassuring picture of God's protection over your life. Just as mountains stand as natural fortresses around Jerusalem, God places Himself as a living shield around His people. His protection is not partial, fragile, or temporary; it is complete, intentional, and unmovable. Mountains represent strength, stability, and permanence. In the same way, God's covering around you is firm and enduring. He surrounds you on every side before you, behind you, above you, and beneath you, ensuring that nothing reaches you without first passing through Him. You are not exposed to danger, forgotten in difficulty, or left vulnerable in uncertain seasons. God's presence is not seasonal or conditional. His protection does not depend on circumstances, emotions, or human strength. From this moment and forevermore, He remains faithful in His watch over your life. Even when you cannot see what He is guarding you from, His hand is actively at work, shielding you from harm and preserving your peace. This reflection invites you to rest. When the Lord surrounds you, fear loses its grip, anxiety is quieted, and confidence rises. You are secure not because of where you stand, but because of who stands around you. God Himself is your defense, your refuge, and your everlasting security.

DELAY DOES NOT
DENY DESTINY!

PRAYER AND DAILY DECLARATION

HEAVENLY Father, I thank You for Your constant presence and unfailing protection over my life. Even in seasons that feel slow, uncertain, or delayed, You remain faithful and intentional. Nothing about my journey is accidental. What feels postponed is not forgotten. What feels delayed is not denied. You are still working, still preparing, and still positioning me according to Your divine purpose. Lord, help me to trust Your timing when progress feels unseen. Guard my heart from discouragement and my mind from doubt. When waiting stretches me, strengthen me. When doors seem closed, remind me that You are aligning what I cannot yet see. My destiny is not fragile; it is secured by Your promise. Today, I decree and declare that delay does not deny my destiny. God's timing is perfect and intentional. I am covered, protected, and positioned by His presence. No opposition can cancel what God has ordained. My steps are guarded, and my future is secured. I refuse to be discouraged by delay. I refuse to measure destiny by the clock. I rest in God's process and trust His preparation. I walk forward in confidence, peace, and assurance, knowing that the God who promised is faithful to fulfill. My life is anchored in His timing, upheld by His power, and guided by His wisdom. In Jesus mighty name, Amen.

SCRIPTURE READING

REFLECTION AND ENCOURAGEMENT

This verse is an invitation into intimacy and security. It does not speak first of protection from danger, but of position dwelling in the secret place. To "dwell" means to remain, to settle, to make your home there. God is not offering occasional shelter; He is inviting you into continual communion. The secret place is not a physical location but a posture of the heart, a life anchored in prayer, trust, and dependence on Him. The "shadow of the Almighty" speaks of closeness. A shadow cannot exist at a distance; it is formed by nearness. When you dwell with God, you live under His covering. His presence becomes your shelter, your defense, and your peace. This is not protection earned by perfection, but protection experienced through relationship. Psalm 91:1 reminds you that safety flows from abiding. When your life is rooted in God's presence, fear loses its dominance and anxiety loses its grip. You are not promised a life without challenges, but you are promised a life under divine covering. There is confidence in knowing that the Most High watches over you, and the Almighty upholds you. To dwell in the secret place means choosing God daily — seeking Him first, trusting Him fully, and remaining near even when life feels uncertain. The reward of dwelling is abiding. You are not temporarily sheltered; you are continuously covered. Let this encourage your heart today: you are invited into closeness with the Almighty. In His presence, you find refuge. Under His shadow, you find peace. When you dwell with Him, you are never exposed or alone, you are securely held beneath the covering of the Most High.

DWELLING UNDER HIS SHADOW!

PRAYER AND DAILY DECLARATION

HEAVENLY Father, I thank You for inviting me into the secret place of Your presence. You are not distant or hidden from me; You welcome me to dwell with You. Teach me to remain close, to abide in trust, and to make my home in Your presence. I choose to dwell with You, not occasionally, but continually. Lord, draw my heart away from distraction and into deeper communion. Let my thoughts rest in You. Let my spirit find peace in Your nearness. When fear tries to rise, remind me that I live under the shadow of the Almighty. When uncertainty surrounds me, anchor me in the assurance that I am covered. Today, I decree and declare that I dwell in the secret place of the Most High. I abide under the shadow of the Almighty. God's presence surrounds and shelters me. I am not exposed or vulnerable. I am covered by divine protection and peace. I remain close to God. I rest in His presence. I live under His constant covering. My heart is steady, my spirit is secure, and my life is anchored in the refuge of the Most High. I walk forward confident, protected, and at peace, knowing that I dwell beneath the shadow of the Almighty. In Jesus mighty name, Amen.

SCRIPTURE READING

Deuteronomy 28:13 "And the LORD shall make thee the head, and not the tail; and thou shalt be above only, and thou shalt not be beneath; if that thou hearken unto the commandments of the LORD thy God, which I command thee this day, to observe and to do them."

REFLECTION AND ENCOURAGEMENT

This scripture is a clear and intentional declaration of God's desire to elevate His people into positions of leadership, influence, and responsibility. God's design for your life is not reactionary but directional. To be "the head" means to lead with wisdom, clarity, and purpose, never from pride, but from stewardship under God's authority. Divine elevation is always connected to obedience. God does not elevate randomly; He positions intentionally. As you align your life with His Word, He lifts you above limitation, confusion, and stagnation. You are not called to live beneath circumstances, fear, or defeat. God's promise declares that you rise not because of your strength alone, but because of His favor and guidance upon your life. To be "above only" means your life is marked by progress rather than regression. Even in seasons of challenge, God sustains forward movement. He sharpens your vision, strengthens your leadership capacity, and orders your steps with purpose. Your elevation is not temporary; it is established by God and reinforced through obedience and faithfulness. As you walk faithfully with Him, your life becomes a reflection of honor, growth, and upward momentum. God's favor rests upon you, empowering you to lead well, influence positively, and fulfill the assignment He has entrusted to you. You are positioned not just to rise but to lead with grace, integrity, and impact.

NOTHING IN MY LIFE IS WASTED!

PRAYER AND DAILY DECLARATION

HEAVENLY Father, I thank You that nothing in my life is accidental or wasted. Every season, every lesson, every challenge, and every victory is being woven together by Your wisdom. Even moments that felt delayed, overlooked, or difficult are being used for my growth and preparation. You are the One who positions, promotes, and establishes me according to Your perfect will. Lord, I trust that elevation comes from You. You refine before You reveal. You prepare before You promote. Teach me to value the process as much as the promise. Let obedience shape my character and humility guard my heart as You lead me into greater responsibility. Today, I decree and declare that nothing in my life is wasted; every season serves a divine purpose. The Lord makes me the head and not the tail. I walk in godly elevation and wise leadership. I am above only and not beneath any circumstance. Obedience positions me for favor and progress. My life reflects growth, honor, and forward movement. God uses every experience to strengthen and prepare me. I receive wisdom to lead with humility, clarity, and grace. Order my steps and establish my path. Cause my life to bring glory to Your name. I embrace responsibility with confidence, knowing that the God who appointed me has also equipped me. In Jesus mighty name, Amen.

SCRIPTURE READING

Genesis 12:2 "And I will make of thee a great nation, and I will bless thee, and make thy name great; and thou shalt be a blessing."

REFLECTION AND ENCOURAGEMENT

This verse reveals the heart of God's blessing. It is intentional, progressive, and purposeful. God does not bless at random, nor does He bless without direction. When He speaks blessing over a life, it carries assignment, responsibility, and generational impact. His promise to Abraham was not merely about increase; it was an invitation into destiny, influence, and legacy. God's blessing enlarges capacity. It stretches vision, strengthens identity, and positions you for significance beyond your present circumstances. To be made "great" in God's eyes is not about pride or recognition; it is about alignment. God elevates those He can trust to steward influence with humility, obedience, and faithfulness. This passage also reminds you that a blessing is never meant to stop with you. God's design is that what He pours into your life, favor, wisdom, resources, and grace, flows outward to others. Your obedience creates ripple effects that touch your family, your community, and even generations you may never meet. Through you, God reveals His goodness in tangible ways. Just as Abraham stepped into a future far greater than what he could see, God is calling you forward. Your life is marked for growth, fruitfulness, and divine impact. As you trust Him and walk in obedience, He establishes your steps, enlarges your capacity, and makes your life a testimony of His faithfulness and purpose.

GOD IS WITH
ME ALWAYS!

PRAYER AND DAILY DECLARATION

HEAVENLY Father, I thank You that You are not distant from my life. You are present, attentive, and actively involved in every step I take. Your presence goes before me, walks beside me, and remains with me through every season. Because You are with me, I am never alone in my responsibilities, my growth, or my calling. I thank You for the intentional blessing You have placed upon my life. What You place in my hands carries purpose, responsibility, and eternal impact. As You enlarge my territory, enlarge my capacity to steward it well. Let my influence reflect Your character. Let my success reflect Your glory. Let my leadership reflect Your wisdom. Today, I decree and declare that God is with me always, His presence establishes my steps, His favor marks my life with purpose. I am blessed and enlarged according to His will. My life carries influence that glorifies God. I am a blessing to my family, my community, and generations after me. I walk boldly into the future God has prepared. I am never unsupported, never abandoned, and never overlooked. Lord, establish my path, expand my vision, and strengthen my heart to steward what You entrust to me. Let everything I do reflect Your presence at work within me. Because You are with me, I move forward in confidence, humility, and assurance. In Jesus mighty name, Amen.

SCRIPTURE READING

Job 22:29 "When men are cast down, then thou shalt say, there is lifting up; and he shall save the humble person."

REFLECTION AND ENCOURAGEMENT

This verse reveals a powerful truth about God's nature. He is the lifter of the humble and the restorer of the discouraged. While circumstances, opinions, or seasons may attempt to define you by loss, limitation, or defeat, God grants you the authority to speak a different word. Even in moments of casting down, He invites you to declare hope and proclaim lifting. God's response to humility is divine intervention. Humility does not mean weakness; it is a posture of trust that positions you to receive God's help. When you remain surrendered to Him, low seasons do not become permanent places. Instead, they become platforms where God's saving power is revealed. He does not overlook the humble heart. He draws near, strengthens it, and restores what feels weary or broken. This scripture also reminds you that what others may perceive as an ending, God sees as a turning point. Setbacks are not signs of abandonment; they are opportunities for God to demonstrate His faithfulness and power. When the world says "cast down," God empowers you to declare, "There is lifting up. "Your present circumstances do not have the final word. God's declaration over your life is restoration, elevation, and hope. As you align your heart with humility and faith, God lifts you, renews your strength, and transforms challenges into testimonies of His grace.

I CARRY POWER, LOVE, AND CLARITY!

PRAYER AND DAILY DECLARATION

HEAVENLY Father, I thank You that You are the lifter of my head and the restorer of my hope. When I feel pressed down, weary, or discouraged, You remind me that I am not powerless. Through Your Spirit, I carry power to overcome, love to respond with grace, and clarity to walk in wisdom. What You have placed within me is greater than what stands before me. Lord, when pressure rises, let power rise within me. When offense tempts my heart, let love govern my response. When confusion tries to cloud my thinking, let clarity settle my mind. Teach me to speak faith instead of fear and to declare Your truth over every circumstance. Today, I decree and declare that I carry power through the Spirit of God. I respond in love, not in fear or frustration. My mind is clear, disciplined, and anchored in truth. There is lifting up for me in every season. God raises me above limitation and discouragement. Every setback becomes a testimony of grace. Restoration and elevation are unfolding in my life. Breakthrough follows obedience and faith. I walk in humility, yet I move in authority. I receive divine help from the Lord and trust Him to lift me, strengthen me, and lead me forward. I embrace the future with confidence, knowing that I am empowered, guided, and upheld by the faithful hand of my God. In Jesus mighty name, Amen.

SCRIPTURE READING

Proverbs 16:24 "Pleasant words are as an honeycomb, sweet to the soul, and health to the bones."

REFLECTION AND ENCOURAGEMENT

This verse reveals the sacred power God has placed within words. Speech is not neutral; it carries the ability to heal or harm, to build or break, to restore or diminish. God designed words to be vessels of life, capable of reaching places that physical touch cannot. When spoken with love, wisdom, and truth, words nourish the soul and bring strength even to the deepest parts of our being. Pleasant words are described as honeycomb, sweet, sustaining, and healing. This imagery reminds us that encouragement, kindness, and grace are not merely emotional comforts; they are spiritual nourishment. The words you speak over yourself and others have the power to revive weary hearts, calm anxious minds, and bring renewal to broken places. As you align your speech with God's heart, your words become instruments of peace and restoration. What you consistently speak shapes your inner world and influences the atmosphere around you. Language rooted in faith, gratitude, and truth releases healing and invites God's presence into everyday moments. This reflection calls you to intentional speech. Choose words that strengthen rather than weaken, heal rather than wound, and reflect God's love rather than fear. Your words are seeds when planted in faith; they produce life, health, and restoration.

WORDS RELEASE HEALING!

PRAYER AND DAILY DECLARATION

HEAVENLY Father, I thank You for the gift of words and the authority You have placed within them. You spoke creation into existence, and You have entrusted me with the power to speak life, truth, and encouragement. Help me to recognize that my words carry weight, shaping my thoughts, influencing my atmosphere, and affecting the hearts of others. Teach me to speak in alignment with Your heart, Your truth, and Your love. Guard my mouth from careless speech, negativity, and doubt. When emotions rise, give me wisdom to pause and choose words that build rather than tear down. Let my language reflect faith instead of fear and hope instead of discouragement. Today, I decree and declare that my words are pleasant, life-giving, and full of grace. My speech brings healing to my soul and strength to my body. I speak wisdom over my decisions, kindness in my interactions, and encouragement into every environment I enter. I declare truth over my circumstances and faith over my future. I decree and declare that my words align with God's truth and purpose. Through my speech, peace flows, and restoration takes root. My mouth is a source of blessing. My conversations reflect Your goodness. My declarations release healing wherever they are spoken. Holy Spirit governs my tongue and guides my conversations. Let every word I speak produce good and lasting fruit. May my speech testify to the transforming power of Your presence within me. In Jesus mighty name, Amen.

SCRIPTURE READING

Isaiah 60:15 "Whereas thou hast been forsaken and hated, so that no man went through thee, I will make thee an eternal excellency, a joy of many generations."

REFLECTION AND ENCOURAGEMENT

This verse is a profound declaration of God's restorative power and redemptive heart. It speaks directly to seasons marked by abandonment, rejection, invisibility, or neglect, times when it felt as though you were overlooked, dismissed, or forgotten. God does not minimize those seasons; instead, He acknowledges them and boldly declares that they will not define the outcome of your life. What once felt empty or desolate becomes the very place where God releases transformation. The Lord specializes in turning sorrow into significance and loss into lasting beauty. He takes what was ignored and reshapes it into something honorable and enduring. Your pain is not erased; it is redeemed, infused with purpose, and woven into a testimony that reflects God's faithfulness and power. To be called an eternal excellency means that God's work in your life will not be temporary or shallow. His restoration carries permanence, dignity, and divine intention. What he rebuilds will stand the test of time. The healing He brings reaches deeper than emotional relief; it establishes identity, restores confidence, and repositions you for meaningful impact. This promise also extends beyond you. God declares that your life will become a joy to many generations. The restoration you receive today becomes a blessing for others tomorrow. Shame is not your inheritance; joy is. What once caused grief will now bring celebration, and your story will echo with hope, honor, and blessings long after the pain has passed.

BEAUTY FROM ASHES!

PRAYER AND DAILY DECLARATION

HEAVENLY Father, I thank You that You are the God who restores, redeems, and renews completely. Nothing in my life is beyond Your reach. You have seen every season where I felt forsaken, overlooked, delayed, or forgotten, and You declare that those seasons are not the conclusion of my story. What felt like loss is becoming preparation. What felt like silence is becoming testimony. Lord, I trust Your redemptive power. Where pain once marked my heart, let beauty now emerge. Where disappointment tried to define me, let purpose redefine me. Where shame attempted to silence me, let honor restore my voice. You are not merely repairing what was broken. You are transforming it into something greater than before. Today, I decree and declare that my past pain is being turned into divine beauty. I am no longer forsaken or forgotten. God is making my life an eternal excellence. My story will bring joy to many generations. Restoration and honor replace former sorrow. I receive Your healing in every wounded place. I receive Your honor in place of shame. I receive Your joy as my strength. Let my life reflect Your redemptive power. Let what You restore in me become a testimony of Your goodness and faithfulness. May my journey speak of Your mercy, and may generations see the evidence of Your grace upon my life. I walk forward renewed, restored, and established, confident that what You have redeemed will endure. In Jesus mighty name, Amen.

SCRIPTURE READING

REFLECTION AND ENCOURAGEMENT

This verse is a powerful declaration of God's direct and active involvement in your battles. It reminds you that victory does not come from personal strength, strategy, or resistance alone; it comes from the Lord who stands as your defender. God does not observe your struggles from a distance; He steps into them with authority, precision, and power. Enemies represent opposition in every form visible and unseen, physical and spiritual. They may appear as resistance, intimidation, delay, misunderstanding, or conflict. Yet God promises that whatever rises against you does not have the final word. What confronts you boldly will be confronted more powerfully by the hand of God. The imagery of enemies fleeing "seven ways" speaks of complete defeat and divine confusion. God does not merely stop the attack. He dismantles the strategy behind it. What was organized against you collapses under His authority. This is not a temporary retreat; it is a decisive victory that leaves no room for return. This scripture passage reassures you that you are not surrounded by enemies; your enemies are surrounded by God. His protection forms a shield around your life, your household, your calling, and your destiny. You are not exposed or vulnerable. You are covered, defended, and preserved by the Lord who fights for you and secures your victory.

THE BATTLE
BELONGS TO GOD!

PRAYER AND DAILY DECLARATION

HEAVENLY Father, I thank You that You are my defender, my strong tower, and my unfailing source of victory. You do not leave me to struggle in my own strength or fight battles alone. You rise on my behalf with power, wisdom, and authority that no enemy can withstand. When opposition forms, You stand between me and every threat. Lord, teach me to rest in Your sovereignty instead of reacting in fear. Where anxiety tries to rise, establish peace. Where intimidation attempts to silence me, strengthen my confidence. Remind me that the battles I face are not greater than the God who fights for me. You are my shield, my advocate, and my righteous defender. Today, I decree and declare that the Lord fights my battles for me. Every enemy rising against me is defeated by God's power. Confusion enters the camp of my adversaries. No weapon formed against me shall prosper; God's power surrounds my life on every side. I walk in victory and divine protection. My peace is preserved, my steps are ordered by the Lord. My life is guarded and established. I choose faith over fear and confidence over doubt. I rest in the assurance that no opposition can overturn what You have ordained. My victory is secure, not because of my effort, but because of Your covenant and Your power at work on my behalf. In Jesus mighty name, Amen.

SCRIPTURE READING

Isaiah 40:4 "Every valley shall be exalted, and every mountain and hill shall be made low: and the crooked shall be made straight, and the rough places plain."

REFLECTION AND ENCOURAGEMENT

This verse is a powerful promise of divine realignment and intentional restoration. It reveals a God who is deeply attentive to the details of your journey. He does not overlook the uneven places, the delays, or the seasons that felt misaligned. Every low moment, every obstacle that seemed immovable, and every path that appeared confusing is fully seen by Him. Valleys represent seasons of discouragement, weakness, or feeling unseen. Mountains and hills symbolize resistance, pressure, and challenges that appear too great to overcome. God declares that neither condition is permanent. He lifts what has been pressed down and brings into submission what has stood in the way of your progress. Nothing is too low for Him to raise, and nothing too high for Him to level. The crooked places speak of uncertainty, detours, and moments where clarity was missing. The rough places represent hardship, frustration, and repeated resistance along the way. God promises personal intervention, straightening what was twisted and smoothing what was difficult. His work is not rushed or careless; it is precise, intentional, and perfectly timed. This scripture passage assures you that God is actively preparing your way forward. He is not only removing obstacles. He is aligning your steps with His purpose. What once slowed you down will no longer hinder you. You are stepping into a season where clarity replaces confusion, peace replaces striving, and steady progress replaces delay.

MOUNTAINS BROUGHT LOW!

PRAYER AND DAILY DECLARATION

HEAVENLY Father, I thank You that You are the God of restoration and divine alignment. Nothing in my life escapes Your notice. You see every detail of my journey, the highs and the lows, the valleys and the mountaintops, and You are faithfully at work preparing my path according to Your perfect will. Even when I cannot see the full picture, You are ordering events, aligning circumstances, and positioning me with purpose. Lord, I trust Your sovereign hand. Where there have been valleys of discouragement or delay, lift me by Your strength. Where mountains of resistance or limitation have stood before me, bring them low by Your power. Where my path has felt crooked or uncertain, straighten it through divine wisdom and clear direction. Today, I decree and declare that every valley in my life is being lifted by God's hand, every mountain and obstacle is being brought low, and every crooked path is made straight by divine intervention. Rough places are smoothed by God's wisdom. My life is aligning with heaven's purpose. I walk in clarity instead of confusion. I move in peace instead of pressure. I rest in trust instead of striving. Lord, order my steps and remove every hindrance that does not serve Your will. Align my desires with Your plan and my timing with Yours. Complete what You have begun in me, and lead me forward with confidence, rest, and steady assurance. I trust that Your alignment brings progress, Your restoration brings wholeness, and Your guidance brings lasting peace. In Jesus mighty name, Amen.

SCRIPTURE READING

Psalm 125:3 "For the rod of the wicked shall not rest upon the lot of the righteous; lest the righteous put forth their hands unto iniquity."

REFLECTION AND ENCOURAGEMENT

This verse is a strong assurance of God's protective justice and faithful oversight over your life. It reveals a God who is deeply invested in preserving what He has assigned to the righteous. He does not permit prolonged oppression, ungodly authority, or unjust pressure to remain over your portion. What touches your life is filtered through His wisdom and governed by His purpose. The "rod of the wicked" represents control, intimidation, manipulation, and systems designed to wear down integrity and faith. God declares that such influence is both limited and temporary. He intervenes before pressure can distort purpose or push the righteous into compromise. Your obedience matters deeply to God, and He actively protects your heart, your character, and your destiny. This promise also reveals God's desire for your stability. He understands that prolonged injustice can weary the soul and cloud discernment. For this reason, He establishes divine boundaries around your life. Challenges may arise, but they do not have permission to dominate or define your future. God preserves you so that righteousness remains your foundation and peace governs your steps. You are not at the mercy of wicked systems, unfair authority, or ungodly influence. Your portion is secured by the Lord Himself. He safeguards what belongs to you and ensures that your destiny unfolds according to His will, not under the weight of oppression, but under the covering of His justice and care.

JUSTICE DEFENDS ME!

PRAYER AND DAILY DECLARATION

HEAVENLY Father, I thank You for Your righteous judgment and Your faithful protection over my life. You are just in all Your ways, and You govern my portion with wisdom and integrity. I rest in the assurance that You watch carefully over what You have entrusted to me. You guard my integrity, preserve my calling, and shield my destiny in every season. Lord, I trust that no unjust authority or hidden opposition can override what You have ordained. Where systems seem unfair, and circumstances appear uncertain, You remain my righteous Judge. You see clearly, You act justly, and You defend faithfully. Establish my life on the foundation of righteousness so that my steps are firm and my heart remains pure. Today, I decree and declare that the rod of the wicked shall not rest over my life. My portion is protected and secured by the Lord. Righteousness preserves my heart and directs my path. My destiny is safe in God's hands. Divine justice works on my behalf. Guard my heart from compromise and keep my motives aligned with Your truth. Strengthen me to walk uprightly, even when challenged. Let integrity mark my character and peace anchor my spirit. I trust You to uphold justice in Your perfect timing. I trust You to preserve me under the covering of Your care. I stand secure, confident that my life is established by righteousness and sustained by Your faithful hand. In Jesus mighty name, Amen.

SCRIPTURE READING

Joel 2:25–26 "And I will restore to you the years that the locust hath eaten, the cankerworm, and the caterpillar, and the palmerworm, my great army which I sent among you. And ye shall eat in plenty, and be satisfied, and praise the name of the LORD your God, that hath dealt wondrously with you: and my people shall never be ashamed."

REFLECTION AND ENCOURAGEMENT

These verses carry one of the most comforting and hope-filled promises in Scripture: nothing in your life is beyond God's ability to restore. God does not ignore seasons of loss, delay, disappointment, or hardship. He sees every year affected by struggle, every effort that seemed wasted, and every opportunity that appeared stolen. His response is not condemnation but restoration. God's promise here is deeply intentional. He does not simply restore outcomes. He restores years. This speaks to redeemed time, renewed purpose, and recovered fruit. What was diminished through circumstances, opposition, or seasons beyond your control is not lost forever. God works with precision, reclaiming what appeared broken beyond repair and restoring it with greater depth and meaning. Restoration in God's hands is never empty. It is accompanied by provision and joy. He replaces lack with abundance, dissatisfaction with fullness, and sorrow with praise. God does not restore you quietly. He restores you in a way that brings testimony. Where shame once tried to take root, gratitude and worship now rise. This promise also affirms your dignity. God declares that His people will never be ashamed. Your story does not conclude in regret, loss, or insufficiency. It ends in satisfaction, honor, and renewed joy. God's restoration touches every area of life, spiritual, emotional, relational, and practical, ensuring that your future reflects His faithfulness and that your life becomes a living witness to His wondrous works.

REDEEMED AND RENEWED!

PRAYER AND DAILY DECLARATION

HEAVENLY Father, I thank You for Your promise of complete and intentional restoration. You are not careless with my life, and You do not overlook the seasons that felt empty, delayed, or painful. You have seen every moment of loss, every unanswered prayer, and every disappointment, and You remain faithful to redeem what was taken and renew what was broken. Lord, I trust that nothing has been wasted. Even the years that felt barren are being woven into Your redemptive plan. Where I experienced lack, release abundance. Where there was sorrow, establish joy. Where there was delay, bring divine fulfillment. Let restoration not be partial, but complete, restoring my confidence, my peace, my opportunities, and my hope. Today, I decree and declare that God is restoring every lost season of my life. Abundance, satisfaction, and joy are my portion. Shame is removed and replaced with praise. My story reflects God's wondrous works. I will not be ashamed, for the Lord is faithful to restore what was lost and redeem what was delayed. Renew my hope and strengthen my faith, let my life stand as evidence of Your goodness and provision. Let my testimony encourage others to trust in Your timing. I receive Your restoration with gratitude, humility, and unwavering confidence that what You promise, You faithfully perform. In Jesus mighty name, Amen.

SCRIPTURE READING

REFLECTION AND ENCOURAGEMENT

This verse is a tender, honest prayer that acknowledges a deep spiritual truth: joy is not something we force or fabricate; it is something God restores. The joy of salvation flows from relationship, grace, and the assurance of God's mercy. It is rooted in knowing that you are forgiven, loved, and held by Him, regardless of outward circumstances. There are seasons when joy feels distant. Weariness, disappointment, spiritual fatigue, or prolonged pressure can quietly drain the heart. In those moments, God does not withdraw or rebuke you. Instead, He invites you closer. Psalm 51:12 reveals the heart of a God who restores what has been depleted and renews what has grown faint. God's restoration is both gentle and powerful. He does not merely lift emotions. He strengthens the inner life. His Spirit upholds you, stabilizes your heart, and restores your capacity to rejoice again. This joy is not shallow or temporary; it is a deep assurance anchored in God's presence and sustained by His grace. This passage encourages honest prayer. When you come before God acknowledging your need, He responds with renewal. Joy can overflow again. Strength can return. Your walk with God can be refreshed and sustained by His faithful, restoring Spirit.

JOY RESTORED DAILY!

PRAYER AND DAILY DECLARATION

HEAVENLY Father, I come before You with humility and honesty, acknowledging my need for renewal. You see where I have grown weary, where my joy has felt diminished, and where my strength has been stretched thin. Yet You remain faithful, faithful to restore what has been worn down and to uphold me by the power of Your Spirit. Lord, breathe fresh life into my heart. Where heaviness has settled, lift it by Your presence. Where discouragement has tried to take root, replace it with hope. I release every burden I have carried too long and invite Your restoring grace to refresh my soul. Today, I decree and declare that the joy of the Lord is restored in my life. My spirit is strengthened and upheld by God's presence. Weariness and heaviness are lifted from my heart, Peace settles my mind, and gratitude fills my thoughts. God's Spirit continually sustains and refreshes me. I walk daily in renewed joy and steady confidence. I am not depleted, I am replenished. I am not defeated, I am restored. Restore my joy, renew my strength, and steady my heart. Let Your presence fill me afresh and cause my joy to overflow again. I receive Your renewal with thanksgiving, trusting that Your grace is sufficient for today and every day ahead. In Jesus mighty name, Amen.

SCRIPTURE READING

REFLECTION AND ENCOURAGEMENT

This verse reveals a comforting and hope-filled truth about your walk with God: your journey is progressive, intentional, and marked by increasing clarity. God does not lead His children backward into darkness or confusion. He leads forward step by step into greater understanding, wisdom, and light. Spiritual growth is often quiet and gradual. There are seasons when progress feels slow, when answers seem partial, and when the road ahead is not fully visible. Yet this scripture assures you that even in those moments, light is increasing. With every act of obedience, every prayer, and every step of faith, God brightens the path before you. The "shining light" speaks of direction, confidence, and divine guidance. What may begin as a small glimmer becomes brighter over time as God unfolds His purpose. He is shaping your discernment, strengthening your faith, and preparing you for the fullness of what He has planned without overwhelming you before the time is right. This passage invites you to trust the process. You are not behind, lost, or stagnant. You are advancing under God's careful guidance. The same God who illuminated your first step will continue to lead you until His purpose is fully revealed. Your future is not dim; it is becoming brighter with each day.

GOD'S LIGHT

LEADS ME!

PRAYER AND DAILY DECLARATION

HEAVENLY Father, I thank You for being the light that guides my life. When the path feels uncertain, or the future seems unclear, Your presence brings illumination and direction. You are the One who orders my steps with wisdom, clarity, and peace. I do not walk blindly; I walk led by Your truth. Lord, let Your light shine upon every area of my life, my decisions, my relationships, my calling, and my future. Where confusion once lingered, release clarity. Where doubt once whispered, establish confidence. Where hesitation tried to delay me, infuse me with steady courage. Teach me to trust that even when I cannot see the entire path, You are faithfully guiding each step. Today, I decree and declare that my path is illuminated by the light of God. My life is moving from glory to glory, clarity, wisdom, and direction increase in me daily. My future grows brighter with every step I take. God's purpose unfolds in perfect timing. I release fear, impatience, and uncertainty. I receive peace, trust, and steady growth. I walk confidently toward God's perfect plan for my life. Let Your light continue to shine upon my path until Your purpose is fully revealed in me. I trust Your guidance, rest in Your wisdom, and move forward assured that my steps are established by You. In Jesus mighty name, Amen.

SCRIPTURE READING

REFLECTION AND ENCOURAGEMENT

This verse reveals the depth of God's compassion and the completeness of His redemptive work in your life. God does not deal with you partially. He forgives fully and heals completely. His mercy reaches into every area where sin once brought guilt and where brokenness once brought pain. Nothing about you is overlooked or dismissed in His care. Forgiveness is the doorway to freedom. When God forgives, He removes guilt, shame, and condemnation, restoring your relationship with Him and renewing your sense of identity. You are no longer defined by past mistakes, failures, or regret. God's forgiveness lifts burdens from the soul and creates space for healing, peace, and renewed hope. Healing flows from the same heart of love. God sees every weakness, every wound, and every area where strength has been affected physically, emotionally, and spiritually. His healing power is not limited by time, diagnosis, or circumstance. What feels deep, long-standing, or complicated is not too difficult for Him. This reflection invites you to receive God's mercy without hesitation. As forgiveness settles your heart, healing begins to flow. God restores wholeness from the inside out, renewing your strength and filling your life with peace. His compassion covers you completely, spirit, soul, and body.

FORGIVEN AND WHOLE!

PRAYER AND DAILY DECLARATION

HEAVENLY Father, I thank You for Your mercy, Your steadfast love, and Your unfailing compassion toward me. You do not forgive partially or reluctantly, You forgive completely and restore fully. You see every hidden wound, every regret, and every place where I have fallen short, yet You respond with grace instead of condemnation. Today, I open my heart to receive all that You have promised. I release every burden of guilt, shame, and self-accusation. I refuse to carry what You have already removed. Let the assurance of Your forgiveness settle deeply within my spirit. Let the truth of Your grace silence every lingering voice of condemnation. Today, I decree and declare that I am forgiven by the mercy of God. Every burden of guilt is lifted from my life. My soul is healed and restored by grace, and my body receives healing and renewed strength. I walk in wholeness, freedom, and peace. Restore my strength where I have felt weak. Renew my heart where I have felt weary. Make me whole in every area, spirit, soul, and body. Let Your healing power flow through every part of my life. Where there has been brokenness, bring restoration. Where there has been pain, bring comfort; where there has been heaviness, release joy. I trust in Your unfailing compassion and receive Your restoring work without hesitation. I move forward, forgiven, healed, and fully embraced by Your love. In Jesus mighty name, Amen.

SCRIPTURE READING

REFLECTION AND ENCOURAGEMENT

This passage offers a powerful assurance that a life rooted in God never loses its vitality or purpose. To be planted in the house of the Lord speaks of consistency, commitment, and deep connection to God's presence. Growth in God is not seasonal or fragile; it is sustained by His faithfulness and nourished by His grace. God's promise here defies natural expectations. While the world measures fruitfulness by youth, speed, or visible strength, God declares that those who remain anchored in Him will continue to flourish regardless of age, season, or circumstance. Your fruitfulness is not determined by time or external conditions it is upheld by the unchanging nature of God Himself. Even when others slow down, fade, or lose momentum, God declares endurance over your life. You are not called to burn out or wither away. You are empowered to keep producing fruit, spiritual fruit that deepens your faith, emotional fruit that reflects maturity and peace, and purposeful fruit that blesses others. Your life becomes living evidence of God's righteousness and stability. This reflection invites you to remain rooted. As you stay planted in God's presence, He continually supplies strength, renewal, and endurance. Your flourishing is not forced; it flows naturally from intimacy with Him. Through your life, others will see that the Lord is upright, faithful, and unshakable in every season.

FLOURISHING IN GRACE!

PRAYER AND DAILY DECLARATION

HEAVENLY Father, I thank You that You have planted me in Your presence and established my life upon a firm foundation. I am not drifting or unanchored; I am rooted in You. My growth does not depend on circumstances, applause, or visible progress; it flows from remaining connected to You. Apart from You, I can do nothing, but in You I flourish. Lord, deepen my roots in Your Word and in Your presence. Let my trust grow stronger than my trials. When seasons feel dry, remind me that my source is not the surface, but the living water within. Sustain me with quiet strength and steady endurance. Shape my character so that my fruit reflects Your righteousness and faithfulness. Today, I decree and declare that I am planted in the house of the Lord. My life flourishes by God's presence and grace, and I bear fruit in every season. Strength and endurance are renewed within me daily. My life testifies to God's righteousness. I am not uprooted by pressure; I am not shaken by delay. I am established and steadfast in Him. Refresh my spirit when I grow weary, sustain my purpose when challenges arise. Let my life continually reflect Your goodness, stability, and truth. I receive spiritual vitality, lasting fruitfulness, and unwavering trust in You. In Jesus mighty name, Amen.

SCRIPTURE READING

REFLECTION AND ENCOURAGEMENT

This verse reveals a powerful and reassuring truth about the source of genuine wisdom and understanding. Insight is not limited to age, education, titles, or experience; it flows from the inspiration of the Almighty. God has placed His Spirit within you, and through His Spirit, understanding is released in ways that surpass human logic and natural reasoning. There are seasons in life when answers cannot be found by analysis alone. Decisions may feel weighty, situations unclear, and directions uncertain. In those moments, God does not leave you to struggle on your own. He breathes wisdom into your spirit, illuminating what cannot be understood by intellect alone and bringing clarity where confusion once lingered. The Spirit of God sharpens discernment, gently guiding your thoughts and helping you perceive what truly matters. He reveals truth progressively, aligning your heart and mind with God's will. You are not limited by what you know today, nor are you stagnant in understanding. As you remain open and responsive to God's leading, He continues to instruct you, expand your insight, and refine your perception. This reflection reminds you that wisdom is a living gift continually supplied by God. When you seek Him sincerely, surrender your thoughts, and listen attentively, He grants understanding that brings peace, confidence, and alignment. God's wisdom does not overwhelm or confuse; it settles your heart and directs your steps with assurance.

DIVINE

UNDERSTANDING

PRAYER AND DAILY DECLARATION

HEAVENLY Father, I thank You for placing Your Spirit within me. I acknowledge that true wisdom and lasting understanding do not come from human intellect, experience, or effort alone, but from You, the source of all truth. Your Spirit is my teacher, my guide, and my counselor. I open my heart and mind to the inspiration of the Almighty, trusting that You reveal what I need to know in every season. Lord, quiet every competing voice and calm every anxious thought. Illuminate my mind with clarity and align my perspective with heaven's wisdom. Where I am tempted to rely only on logic or personal reasoning, remind me that Your insight surpasses my understanding. Sharpen my discernment so I can recognize truth, avoid deception, and walk confidently in Your will. Today, I decree and declare that the Spirit of the Lord dwells within me. By the inspiration of the Almighty, I receive wisdom and understanding. My mind is illuminated by divine truth; my discernment is sharpened by God's Spirit. I am guided by heavenly insight and not limited by natural reasoning. My decisions align with God's clarity and peace; my steps are ordered with wisdom. My heart remains sensitive to the leading of the Holy Spirit. I surrender my thoughts, plans, and unanswered questions to You. Lead me by Your Spirit, instruct me with Your wisdom, and establish my path in understanding. Let my life reflect obedience, discernment, and the steady guidance of Your truth. In Jesus mighty name, Amen.

SCRIPTURE READING

REFLECTION AND ENCOURAGEMENT

This verse reveals a profound truth about God's trust and intentional design for humanity. While the heavens remain under God's sovereign rule, He has deliberately entrusted the earth to people. This speaks of responsibility, stewardship, and authority. Your presence on the earth is not accidental. Your life carries an assignment, purpose, and divine trust. God's act of giving reflects partnership. He invites you to participate in His work by managing, influencing, and cultivating what He has created. This stewardship goes beyond ownership; it is about alignment with God's heart. Through wisdom, creativity, and spiritual authority, you are empowered to reflect God's kingdom in practical, everyday ways. This passage also highlights accountability. What God places in your care, your time, talents, relationships, resources, and opportunities, is meant to be stewarded with faithfulness and integrity. When you submit your authority to God, He brings clarity to your decisions and grace to your responsibilities. Faithful stewardship opens the door for increase, impact, and lasting fruit. You are not powerless in your world. God has entrusted you with influence and equipped you to lead, build, and serve well. As you walk in obedience and humility, your stewardship becomes a testimony of God's wisdom at work through your life.

FAITHFUL IN STEWARDSHIP!

PRAYER AND DAILY DECLARATION

HEAVENLY Father, I thank You for trusting me with responsibility and for placing purpose upon my life. Nothing in my hands is accidental. The assignments, resources, relationships, and opportunities You have given me carry eternal significance. What I steward today has the potential to impact tomorrow. I recognize that my life is not my own; it is entrusted to me for Your glory. Lord, give me a heart of faithful stewardship. Teach me to handle influence with humility, authority with wisdom, and responsibility with obedience. Guard me from carelessness and pride. Let integrity guide my decisions, and excellence shape my actions. May my leadership reflect Your character and my service reflect Your love. Today, I decree and declare that I am entrusted with divine stewardship. I walk in authority with humility and discernment. I steward my resources, relationships, and gifts faithfully. My life produces impact and kingdom results. God partners with me to fulfill His purposes on the earth. I manage wisely what You have placed in my hands. I lead responsibly and serve faithfully. I multiply what You entrust to me. Let my life reflect excellence, integrity, and alignment with Your kingdom. Establish my steps, expand my capacity, and strengthen my character as I steward Your purposes well. I choose to be faithful in the small and steadfast in the great, trusting that You are shaping me for lasting impact. In Jesus mighty name, Amen.

SCRIPTURE READING

REFLECTION AND ENCOURAGEMENT

This verse is a powerful promise of restored peace, divine security, and lasting stability. God speaks directly to places that once threatened your borders, boundaries, home, and inner life and declares that disruption, loss, and destruction no longer have authority to remain. What once unsettled your peace is replaced by God's order and protection. The imagery is deeply reassuring. Walls represent protection, defense, and boundaries. God declares that your walls will be called Salvation, meaning your safety is not fragile or dependent on circumstances; it is firmly rooted in God's saving power. Gates represent access: what enters and exits your life. God names your gates Praise, showing that worship, gratitude, and honor to Him now define your atmosphere. This passage reveals that God does more than remove danger. He establishes peace. He rebuilds what was broken, strengthens what was vulnerable, and restores what was threatened. Where fear once guarded the entrance, praise now stands watch. Where instability once ruled, salvation now secures every boundary. As you lift praise at your gates, your heart is renewed, and your environment is transformed. God's peace settles your life, His salvation surrounds you, and worship becomes your response. You are not merely surviving; you are dwelling in a place God Himself has secured.

PEACE WITHIN MY BORDERS!

PRAYER AND DAILY DECLARATION

HEAVENLY Father, I thank You for establishing peace within my life and within my borders. You are not only the giver of peace, but the One who sustains and enforces it. I receive Your salvation as my defense and welcome Your presence to rule over every area of my life, my home, my relationships, my work, and my future. Lord, let Your peace govern my atmosphere. Where turmoil once attempted to enter, establish divine order. Where fear tried to linger, release assurance. I declare that my life is not vulnerable to chaos, for it is covered by Your covenant. You are my protector, my defender, and the keeper of all that concerns me. Today, I decree and declare that violence, waste, and destruction will not be heard in my land. My walls are Salvation, and my gates are Praise. My home and boundaries are secured by God's saving power. Peace is established over my life and household. God's protection surrounds me on every side. My atmosphere is filled with worship, thanksgiving, and joy. Praise guards my entrance, and gratitude strengthens my foundation; salvation stands as my defense and my shield. Guard all that concerns me, Lord. Strengthen my dwelling and preserve my inheritance. Let my life reflect the calm confidence that comes from knowing You reign within my borders. May my heart overflow with praise, and may Your peace remain constant and unshaken over all You have entrusted to me. In Jesus mighty name, Amen.

SCRIPTURE READING

Habakkuk 2:3 "For the vision is yet for an appointed time… though it tarry, wait for it; because it will surely come, it will not tarry."

REFLECTION AND ENCOURAGEMENT

This verse anchors your heart in the truth that God's promises are ruled by divine timing, not human pressure. What God has shown you, whether through prayer, His Word, or quiet assurance, has not been forgotten or delayed by chance. Every vision carries an appointed time, fixed by God Himself, and that timing is always purposeful. Waiting can feel uncomfortable, especially when anticipation is high and circumstances appear unchanged. Yet Scripture reminds us that waiting is not stagnation; it is preparation. While fulfillment may seem slow, God is actively at work aligning people, shaping character, strengthening faith, and preparing you for what is ahead. The promise is moving, even when progress feels invisible. This passage teaches patience that is rooted in trust. God assures us that His word will speak clearly and truthfully at the right moment. It will not fail, arrive prematurely, or miss its season. The waiting period refines endurance and deepens dependence on God rather than on outcomes. So take courage. You are not behind schedule, overlooked, or forgotten. God's timing is precise, and His promises are dependable. What He has spoken over your life will surely come to pass, and when it does, it will arrive exactly when it should, complete, purposeful, and right on time.

VISION WILL MANIFEST!

PRAYER AND DAILY DECLARATION

HEAVENLY Father, I thank You for every vision and promise You have spoken over my life. Not one word from You falls to the ground. What You declare carries power, purpose, and fulfillment within it. I recognize that Your timing is perfect and that You are faithful to complete what You have begun in me. Even when I cannot see immediate results, I trust that You are working behind the scenes, aligning circumstances and preparing me for manifestation. Lord, teach me to wait well. Guard my heart from discouragement and impatience. Let hope anchor my soul while I stand in expectation. Where doubt attempts to whisper delay, remind me that Your promises are not postponed, they are unfolding. Today, I decree and declare that God's promises over my life are alive and active. Waiting does not mean denial. The vision will speak and will not lie. What God has promised will surely come to pass; divine timing governs my fulfillment. I wait with patience, faith, and steady confidence. I choose trust over frustration and faith over fear. My hope remains anchored in God's faithfulness. Strengthen my heart as I wait. Steady my spirit with assurance. Align my character with the promise and prepare me for what You are bringing forth. I remain confident that in Your perfect time, every word You have spoken will manifest fully and clearly. In Jesus mighty name, Amen.

SCRIPTURE READING

REFLECTION AND ENCOURAGEMENT

This verse is a firm and comforting declaration of God's protective authority over your life and your household. It establishes clear spiritual boundary lines that danger cannot cross and harm cannot penetrate. God Himself speaks protection, and when He declares safety, no opposing force has permission to override His word. In seasons where fear may attempt to rise through troubling reports, uncertainty, or unseen threats, this promise stands as a shield. God does not merely reduce risk; He forbids evil from prevailing. Your dwelling is marked by His presence, and where God's presence abides, peace is established, and fear is displaced. God's protection is not passive or occasional. It is deliberate, constant, and personal. He watches over you day and night, guarding your steps and preserving your home. Even when you are unaware of what He is preventing, His hand is actively at work blocking harm, redirecting danger, and maintaining peace within your borders. This promise invites you to rest. You are not exposed or vulnerable; you are kept. Your life and your household are under divine care, secured by a faithful God whose word does not waver. Let this truth quiet your heart and anchor your confidence as you trust Him fully.

DIVINE PROTECTION, DIVINE PEACE!

PRAYER AND DAILY DECLARATION

HEAVENLY Father, I thank You for Your faithful covering over my life and over my household. You are not distant or unaware that You are present, attentive, and actively guarding all that concerns me. I choose to trust Your Word and rest in the security You provide. Your promises are not fragile; they are firm and established. Lord, I declare that my dwelling is not exposed to harm or chaos. Your presence rests upon my home as a shield and a sanctuary. Where fear has attempted to enter, I replace it with trust. Where anxiety has tried to linger, I receive Your peace. Let Your angels stand guard, and Your Spirit fill every room with calm assurance. Today, I decree and declare that no evil shall befall me, no plague shall come near my dwelling. My home is covered by God's presence, peace, and safety surrounds my household. Divine protection establishes my borders. I rest securely under God's protection. I release fear and embrace peace, my steps are preserved, and my path is guarded. Guard my home, Lord. Preserve my steps and the steps of those I love. Let Your presence continually fill my dwelling with calm, safety, and confidence. May my household be marked by worship, stability, and divine covering in every season. In Jesus mighty name, Amen.

SCRIPTURE READING

REFLECTION AND ENCOURAGEMENT

This verse is a powerful reminder that God never assigns purpose without also providing power. You were never meant to live timidly, uncertainly, or dependent solely on your own strength. God promises supernatural empowerment through the Holy Spirit so that you can live boldly, intentionally, and effectively in the life He has called you to. The power spoken here is not merely emotional strength or motivation; it is divine enablement. The Holy Spirit equips you with clarity, courage, discernment, and endurance. He strengthens you to stand firm in truth, to walk confidently in obedience, and to navigate life with spiritual authority. You are not left to figure things out alone; God's Spirit actively works within you. This passage also redefines what it means to be a witness. Witnessing is not confined to sermons or stages; it is revealed through how you live, speak, love, and respond. Wherever God places you, your home, workplace, community, or unfamiliar spaces, your life becomes a living testimony of His grace and power. Your consistency, integrity, and faith quietly point others toward Christ. You do not rely on talent alone or human approval. The Holy Spirit empowers you to represent Christ with authenticity and confidence. As you yield to Him, your life carries influence that extends beyond what you can see. God's power working through you ensures that your purpose is fulfilled and your witness leaves a lasting impact.

EMPOWERED BY THE SPIRIT!

PRAYER AND DAILY DECLARATION

HEAVENLY Father, I thank You for the gift of the Holy Spirit and for the divine power You have placed within me. I acknowledge that I am not designed to live by human strength alone, but by the strength and enabling grace that comes from You. Your Spirit is not distant or symbolic. He is active within me, empowering, guiding, and sustaining me daily. Lord, awaken me to the power that already dwells within me. Where I have felt inadequate, remind me that I am equipped, where I hesitated, release boldness. Where fear has tried to silence me, establish courage. Let me not shrink back from purpose, but step forward in confidence, knowing You go with me. Today, I decree and declare that I receive power through the Holy Spirit, and I walk boldly in my God-given calling. My life is a witness to God's truth, love, and grace. I am equipped for purpose, impact, and obedience. I represent Christ with clarity, courage, and humility. I am not powerless, I am empowered. I am not alone; I am accompanied by Your Spirit. I am not uncertain; I am guided by divine wisdom. Fill me afresh with Your Spirit. Strengthen my heart to remain faithful, guide my steps with discernment, and let my life reflect Your presence wherever I go. Use me as a vessel of hope, truth, and light in every place You send me. In Jesus mighty name, Amen.

SCRIPTURE READING

Numbers 6:24–26 "The LORD bless thee and keep thee: The LORD make his face shine upon thee, and be gracious unto thee: The LORD lift up his countenance upon thee, and give thee peace."

REFLECTION AND ENCOURAGEMENT

This passage is one of the most tender and powerful expressions of God's heart toward His people. It reveals that God's blessing is not distant or abstract; it is personal, intentional, and actively spoken over your life. To be blessed by the Lord means to be empowered by His goodness, sustained by His care, and surrounded by His presence. God's promise to keep you speaks of protection and preservation. He watches over your life with attentiveness, guarding what concerns you and ensuring that nothing entrusted to Him is lost. You are not left to fend for yourself; you are carefully kept by a faithful God who neither sleeps nor forgets. The shining of God's face represents approval, grace, and nearness. It means God is attentive to you, inclined toward you with love, and involved in your journey. When His countenance is lifted upon you, it brings assurance that you are seen, valued, and favored not because of perfection, but because of relationship. This blessing culminates in peace, a deep, sustaining peace that settles the heart and steadies the soul. It is not dependent on circumstances but rooted in God's presence. Where God's blessing rests, fear diminishes, anxiety loosens its grip, and wholeness is restored. This passage invites you to receive God's blessing daily, knowing that His favor surrounds you and His peace anchors your life.

THE LORD BLESSES AND KEEPS ME!

PRAYER AND DAILY DECLARATION

HEAVENLY Father, I receive Your blessing with gratitude and faith. I thank You that Your blessing is not temporary or conditional, but intentional and sustaining. You are attentive to my life, mindful of my needs, and faithful to keep me by Your power. Your watchful care surrounds me, and Your peace settles over me like a covering. Lord, let the assurance of Your blessing quiet every fear and silence every doubt. When uncertainty arises, remind me that I am kept by You. When challenges appear, anchor my heart in the truth that Your hand rests upon my life. Your favor is not accidental; it is purposeful. Your grace is not limited; it is abundant. Today, I decree and declare that the Lord blesses me and keeps me. God's face shines upon me with grace and favor. I walk under divine approval and protection. Peace is established in my heart, my home, and my path. My life is guarded and sustained by God's presence. I am not just striving for blessings; I am resting in them. I am not seeking security; I am kept by His power. I am not unsettled, I am established in peace. Let Your grace mark my days, and Your favor surround every step I take. May Your peace rule my thoughts and steady my spirit. I rest confidently in Your blessing, trust fully in Your keeping, and receive the peace You freely give. In Jesus mighty name, Amen.

SCRIPTURE READING

REFLECTION AND ENCOURAGEMENT

This verse reveals God's heart for your life to be marked by overflow, not exhaustion. Faith in Christ is not meant to leave you empty, striving, or spiritually dry. When you believe in Him, God places a living, active source within you, one that continually refreshes, renews, and sustains. The "rivers of living water" speak of the Holy Spirit flowing freely from within. Rivers are not stagnant; they move, nourish, and bring life wherever they go. This means God's work in you is not meant to stop with you. What He pours into your spirit is designed to flow outward, bringing encouragement, healing, wisdom, and hope to those around you. Even in seasons that feel dry, demanding, or overwhelming, this promise remains true. Your source is not external circumstances but an internal supply from God Himself. You may feel stretched, but you are never emptied. God refreshes you from within, strengthening your faith and renewing your joy day by day. This scripture reminds you that overflow is not earned; it flows from belief. As you trust Christ, His Spirit continues to work through you, causing your life to reflect vitality, grace, and spiritual abundance. You are not merely sustained; you are empowered to be a blessing.

RIVERS OF LIVING WATER FLOW!

PRAYER AND DAILY DECLARATION

HEAVENLY Father, I thank You that through faith in Christ, You have placed living water within me. I am not sustained by my own strength, but by the continual flow of Your Spirit. You are the source of my renewal, and You never run dry. Even when circumstances feel draining, Your Spirit remains a wellspring within me. Lord, I receive the refreshing and renewing work of Your Spirit in every area of my life. Where there has been weariness, release vitality. Where there has been dryness, release overflow. Where discouragement has tried to settle, let Your living water rise within me and wash it away. Today, I decree and declare that rivers of living water flow through my life. I am continually refreshed by the Holy Spirit. I will not live depleted, weary, or spiritually dry. God's life flows through me to bless others. I walk in overflow, faith, and spiritual vitality. I am not empty, I am filled. I am not stagnant, I am flowing. I am not exhausted, I am renewed. Fill me afresh, Lord. Let Your Spirit flow freely within me and through me. May my words, actions, and presence carry refreshment to those around me. Let my life bring encouragement, healing, and hope wherever You lead me. In Jesus mighty name, Amen.

SCRIPTURE READING

Galatians 3:13 "Christ hath redeemed us from the curse of the law, being made a curse for us… for it is written, Cursed is every one that hangeth on a tree."

REFLECTION AND ENCOURAGEMENT

This verse proclaims one of the most powerful truths of the Gospel: your freedom has already been paid for. Redemption is not a theory or a hope; it is a finished work. Christ stepped into your place, took upon Himself what was meant to bind you, and completed the exchange at the cross. What once carried weight, judgment, and accusation no longer has authority over your life. To be redeemed means you were bought back with intention and love. Jesus did not merely cover sin; He broke its power. Every curse spoken, inherited, generational, or self-inflicted was addressed fully through Christ's sacrifice. The law's demands were satisfied, and its penalties were silenced. You are no longer defined by failure, guilt, or limitation. This scripture also reveals the doorway to blessing. Redemption does not leave you empty; it repositions you. Through Christ, you move from curse to blessing, from bondage to freedom, from striving to grace. Your identity is restored, your standing before God is secure, and your access to His promises is open. Freedom in Christ is not something you earn daily; it is something you stand in confidently. Your past no longer dictates your future. Your life is now shaped by what Christ has accomplished, not by what once held you captive. You are redeemed, restored, and released to live fully under God's blessing.

OVERFLOW

WITHOUT LIMIT!

PRAYER AND DAILY DECLARATION

HEAVENLY Father, I thank You that through Christ, I am not a container of limitation but a carrier of living water. Your Spirit dwells within me as a mighty, unstoppable flow. I am not dependent on circumstances for renewal; heaven's supply lives inside me. What You have placed within me cannot be dried up by pressure, opposition, or delay. Lord, let every dormant place within me come alive. Where there has been stagnation, release movement. Where there has been drought, release overflow. Where the enemy attempted to drain my strength, let Your Spirit surge with greater force. I refuse to live beneath what You have deposited in me. I will not shrink back into dryness when You have called me to overflow. Today, I decree and declare that rivers of living water surge through me. The Spirit of God flows powerfully within me. Every dry place in my life is revived, weariness is broken. Spiritual stagnation is uprooted. I am not empty, I overflow. I am not depleted, I am replenished. I am not stagnant; I am moving in divine momentum. Let Your Spirit break forth in me like a flood. Let renewal spring up suddenly. Let revival begin in my own heart and spill into every environment I enter. May my presence carry life. May my words release hope. May my obedience unlock breakthrough. I declare that what flows in me will flow through me, refreshing the weary, strengthening the weak, and revealing the power of God. I am a vessel of living water, and heaven's current runs strong within me. In Jesus mighty name, Amen.

SCRIPTURE READING

REFLECTION AND ENCOURAGEMENT

This verse unveils a powerful spiritual reality: through Christ, you are not confined to natural thinking or limited perception. You have access to divine wisdom. God's perspective, priorities, and peace. The mind of Christ enables you to discern truth, respond with grace, and navigate life with clarity that transcends circumstance. When uncertainty presses in or decisions feel weighty, this promise anchors your heart. You are not left to figure things out alone. The Holy Spirit within you illuminates understanding, aligns your thoughts with God's truth, and steadies your emotions. What feels confusing can become clear; what feels overwhelming can be approached with calm confidence. Having the mind of Christ means your thinking is continually renewed. Old patterns of fear, doubt, or anxiety lose their grip as God reshapes your perspective. You begin to see situations through faith rather than fear, hope rather than despair, and wisdom rather than impulse. Your responses reflect Christ's humility, patience, and love. This reflection invites you to lean into revelation. Wisdom is not distant, it is present and accessible. As you submit your thoughts to God, He grants insight, direction, and peace, empowering you to walk in alignment with His will.

I HAVE THE MIND OF CHRIST!

PRAYER AND DAILY DECLARATION

HEAVENLY Father, I thank You that through Christ I have access to divine wisdom and understanding. I am not left to navigate life by human reasoning alone. You have given me the mind of Christ, and through Your Spirit, I can think, discern, and respond in alignment with heaven. Lord, renew my mind daily. Where old patterns of fear, doubt, or insecurity attempt to linger, replace them with truth and clarity. Align my thoughts with Your Word and my perspective with Your purpose. Guard my mind from confusion and distraction. Let peace rule my thinking and wisdom shape my decisions. Today, I decree and declare that I have the mind of Christ. My thoughts are guided by God's wisdom and truth. Clarity replaces confusion in every area of my life. My decisions are led by the Holy Spirit. Understanding and discernment increase within me. I think clearly, I respond wisely, I move forward in peace, I submit my mind to You, Lord. Shape my perspective and guard my thoughts from negativity and deception. Let Your wisdom guide every choice I make and every word I speak. May my thinking reflect faith, maturity, and spiritual insight. I walk confidently, knowing that Your Spirit illuminates my understanding and establishes my steps. In Jesus mighty name, Amen.

SCRIPTURE READING

Judges 6:12 "And the angel of the LORD appeared unto him, and said unto him, The LORD is with thee, thou mighty man of valour."

REFLECTION AND ENCOURAGEMENT

This verse reveals a powerful truth about how God sees you. When the angel spoke these words to Gideon, Gideon was not standing boldly on a battlefield; he was hiding, uncertain, and afraid. Yet God addressed him according to destiny, not circumstance. This teaches us that God speaks identity before evidence appears. He calls out what He has placed inside you, even when you cannot yet see it yourself. God's declaration over Gideon was rooted in His presence: "The Lord is with thee." Strength is not self-generated; it flows from divine companionship. Where you may feel inadequate, hesitant, or overwhelmed, God's presence redefines your capacity. His presence supplies courage, wisdom, and endurance for the task ahead. This passage also reassures us that calling comes before confidence. God does not wait for you to feel ready. He walks with you as you grow into what He has spoken. Every step of obedience invites greater strength. Every response of faith activates divine help. What begins in weakness matures into boldness through God's sustaining presence. Be encouraged today: you are not unseen, unqualified, or forgotten. God is with you. And because He is with you, you are stronger than fear, greater than limitation, and fully equipped for the assignment He has entrusted to you.

ENABLED BY GRACE!

PRAYER AND DAILY DECLARATION

HEAVENLY Father, I thank You for Your abiding presence in my life. You do not send me into purpose alone. You walk with me, strengthen me, and sustain me. Your presence is not seasonal or conditional; it is constant and faithful. Because You are with me, I am never without help, direction, or support. Lord, I receive the identity You have spoken over me. I am not defined by fear, past mistakes, or insecurity. I am defined by Your calling and Your grace. Strengthen me for every assignment You have placed in my hands. Where I feel inadequate, remind me that You are sufficient. Where hesitation rises, establish courage. Today, I decree and declare that the Lord is with me. I am strong in God and called for a purpose, fear does not define or limit me, courage rises within me, and faith governs my steps. God equips me fully to fulfill my calling. I am prepared for what lies ahead. I move in obedience and confidence. I step forward trusting Your presence to guide me, Your strength to sustain me, and Your purpose to unfold through my life. What You have called me to do, You have empowered me to accomplish. I walk boldly, knowing that You go before me and remain beside me. In Jesus mighty name, Amen.

SCRIPTURE READING

REFLECTION AND ENCOURAGEMENT

This verse reminds us that words are not neutral; they carry weight, influence, and direction. God calls you to speak with grace, not merely politeness, but divine kindness rooted in wisdom and truth. Grace-filled speech reflects the heart of God and has the power to heal wounds, calm tension, and create understanding even in difficult moments. Speech "seasoned with salt" speaks of discernment and wisdom. Just as salt preserves and enhances flavor, wisdom gives your words depth, balance, and clarity. God desires that your responses be thoughtful rather than reactive, intentional rather than careless. Even when conversations are challenging, He equips you to respond with insight and restraint. God is attentive not only to what you say, but also to how you say it. Tone, timing, and intention matter. When the Holy Spirit guides your speech, your words become instruments of peace rather than division, encouragement rather than discouragement, and truth rather than confusion. This passage invites you to be intentional with your words. As you lean on God daily, your speech becomes aligned with His heart. Your voice carries wisdom, your responses reflect grace, and your words open doors instead of closing them.

SPEAKING WITH GRACE!

PRAYER AND DAILY DECLARATION

HEAVENLY Father, I thank You for the wisdom You place within me and for the steady guidance of Your Spirit. You care not only about what I do, but about what I say. My words carry influence, shape atmospheres, and impact hearts. Teach me to speak with grace, clarity, and love in every situation, especially when emotions rise or pressure increases. Lord, let my speech be governed by maturity and discernment. When I am tempted to react, teach me to respond. When conversations grow tense, anchor me in peace. Guard my tongue from haste, harshness, and negativity. Fill my heart so fully with Your truth that what flows from my mouth reflects Your character. Today, I decree and declare that my speech is filled with grace. My words are seasoned with wisdom and discernment. I speak with clarity, kindness, and understanding. My words bring peace, healing, and encouragement. My speech honors God and reflects His heart. I will not speak carelessly. I will not respond from emotion alone. I will speak life and truth in love. Let my words build where there has been brokenness, restore where there has been hurt, and bless wherever they are spoken. Guard my mouth, guide my responses, and let everything I say bring glory to You. May my conversations reflect maturity, my tone reflect compassion, and my language reflect faith. In Jesus mighty name, Amen.

SCRIPTURE READING

Psalm 54:4 "Behold, God is mine helper: the Lord is with them that uphold my soul."

REFLECTION AND ENCOURAGEMENT

This verse offers deep reassurance that help is not distant or abstract. God Himself is your helper. When strength feels limited and burdens feel heavy, the Lord does not stand on the sidelines. He steps in personally to uphold, sustain, and strengthen you from within. God's help is intimate and intentional. He supports your soul, the place of emotions, thoughts, and inner endurance. When weariness settles in or discouragement tries to take root, God lifts the weight you were never meant to carry alone. His presence restores courage, renews hope, and steadies your heart. This passage also reveals that God's help often comes layered. He is with those who uphold your soul, His Spirit, His grace, and sometimes the people He assigns to walk with you. Support is part of God's design. You are not weak for needing help; you are wise for receiving what God provides. So take comfort in this truth: when you feel weary, God is lifting you. When you feel overwhelmed, God is sustaining you. His help is constant, His support is faithful, and His strength never fails.

GOD IS MY HELPER!

PRAYER AND DAILY DECLARATION

HEAVENLY Father, I thank You for being my ever-present helper and the One who faithfully upholds my soul. You are not distant from my needs or unaware of my burdens. In moments of weakness, You strengthen me. In times of uncertainty, You steady me. I rest in Your sustaining power and trust Your unwavering support over my life. Lord, remind me that I am never alone. When I feel stretched or overwhelmed, anchor my heart in the truth that You stand beside me. Uphold my soul when it feels weary. Guard my mind when doubts attempt to arise. Let Your presence be my constant reassurance and my secure foundation. Today, I decree and declare that God is my helper, the Lord upholds my soul. I am strengthened by God's presence. I am not alone or unsupported. Divine help surrounds my life. I receive Your help with gratitude and faith. I rely on Your strength instead of my own. I move forward sustained by Your grace. Uphold me, Lord, in every season, whether in quiet growth or visible challenge. Strengthen my inner being, steady my steps, and sustain my purpose. Let my life reflect the confidence of one who knows that heaven's help is near. In Jesus mighty name, Amen.

SCRIPTURE READING

REFLECTION AND ENCOURAGEMENT

This passage beautifully reveals the precision and faithfulness of God's provision. God not only promised to sustain Elijah. He gave him specific instructions. Provision was tied to obedience, and supply was released in the place God assigned him to dwell. Elijah's responsibility was not to figure out how provision would come, but to trust where God sent him. God knows exactly where to sustain you. Sometimes provision flows in places that seem hidden, quiet, or unexpected by a brook, away from crowds, outside familiar systems. Yet those places are not signs of lack; they are places of divine care. When God positions you, He also plans your supply. This passage reminds us that God's provision is not always conventional, but it is always intentional. Ravens— unlikely carriers became vessels of daily sustenance. Morning and evening, consistently and faithfully, God met Elijah's needs. This shows that God's supply is not random or delayed; it is timely, sufficient, and reliable. Obedience unlocks alignment. When you follow God's direction, even when it doesn't fully make sense, you place yourself under His provision. God sees your needs, knows your season, and commands supply to meet you exactly where you are. You are not forgotten, misplaced, or overlooked; you are sustained by divine design.

PROVISION MEETS OBEDIENCE!

PRAYER AND DAILY DECLARATION

HEAVENLY Father, I thank You for being my faithful Provider and Sustainer. You are not limited by circumstances, economies, or human systems. You are the source of every good and perfect gift, and You care intimately about every detail of my life. I trust You to meet my needs as I walk in obedience to Your Word and follow Your leading with faith. Lord, teach me to rely on You daily. Remove every trace of anxiety about provision and replace it with confidence in Your care. Where fear tries to whisper lack, let faith declare abundance. Where uncertainty attempts to distract me, anchor me in the truth that You supply with wisdom and precision. Today, I decree and declare that God supplies all my needs according to His wisdom and care. Obedience positions me for divine provision. I am sustained daily by God's faithfulness. Divine supply meets me exactly where God has placed me. My life is upheld by the unfailing provision of the Lord. I will not strive in fear, I will not doubt in uncertainty and I will trust and obey. Where You lead me, You will sustain me fully. Where You assign me, You will equip me completely. I rest in the assurance that Your provision is timely, sufficient, and intentional. In Jesus mighty name, Amen.

SCRIPTURE READING

REFLECTION AND ENCOURAGEMENT

This verse is a beautiful proclamation of divine restoration and re-identity. God does not merely repair what was broken. He renames it. What once carried the label Forsaken is now called Hephzibah, meaning "My delight is in her." What was once Desolate is now called Beulah, meaning "married" or "belonging." This is not a surface change; it is covenant restoration. God addresses the pain of abandonment, rejection, and silence with intentional love. He removes the names shaped by loss and replaces them with names formed by His delight. This reveals a deep truth: God does not define you by what you went through. He defines you by what He has spoken over you. To be called Hephzibah means you are not merely accepted, you are enjoyed. God takes pleasure in you. He is emotionally invested in your restoration and committed to your future. Areas of your life that once felt empty or disconnected are now being brought into alignment, union, and fruitfulness under His hand. This passage reassures you that your story is not ending in desolation. God is rewriting it with honor, belonging, and joy. Your identity is no longer shaped by what was lost, but by the One who delights in you. You are restored, renamed, and reclaimed by God Himself.

HEPHZIBAH – THE LORD DELIGHTS IN ME!

PRAYER AND DAILY DECLARATION

HEAVENLY Father, I thank You for restoring not only my circumstances, but my identity. You do not merely change what surrounds me. You transform who I understand myself to be. Where labels of rejection, failure, or abandonment once tried to define me, You speak a new name over my life. I receive the name You have declared and the delight You have spoken concerning me. Lord, let the truth of my identity in Christ take root deeply within my heart. I am not forgotten. I am not overlooked. I am chosen, cherished, and called. Where desolation once marked my story, restoration now rises. Where emptiness once lingered, purpose now flourishes. Today, I decree and declare that I am no longer forsaken or abandoned. The Lord delights in me; every desolate area of my life is restored. My identity is renewed and established in Christ. My future is filled with promise, joy, and belonging. I embrace my new name. I stand confidently in my restored place. I walk securely in my covenant position with You. Let my life reflect Your delight and Your redeeming love. May my confidence come from knowing I am fully known and fully loved by You. Establish me in truth, anchor me in belonging, and let my story testify to Your faithfulness across generations. In Jesus mighty name, Amen.

SCRIPTURE READING

REFLECTION AND ENCOURAGEMENT

This verse reveals the spiritual power of remembrance and intentional celebration in the life of a believer. God instructed His people to mark significant moments, days of joy, solemn occasions, and new beginnings not with silence or haste, but with deliberate worship. These moments were to be acknowledged before God, transforming ordinary days into sacred milestones. Remembrance is not about living in the past; it is about anchoring the present in God's faithfulness. When you pause to remember what God has done, you realign your heart with truth and strengthen your confidence for what lies ahead. God wanted His people to mark their seasons so they would never forget that every victory, transition, and new chapter was rooted in His presence. This passage also teaches us that praise invites divine favor. When worship rises intentionally, especially at the beginning of a season, it establishes a spiritual memorial before God. It declares, "Lord, You were here before, and You are here again." Gratitude becomes a spiritual language that honors God and invites His continued guidance, peace, and blessing. As you move forward, let your life be marked by intentional remembrance. Celebrate God in your gladness, acknowledge Him in transitions, and welcome Him into every new beginning. When remembrance becomes your rhythm, joy deepens, faith strengthens, and divine favor follows your steps.

JOY IN EVERY SEASON!

PRAYER AND DAILY DECLARATION

HEAVENLY Father, I thank You for walking with me through every season of my life, the seasons of growth and the seasons of waiting, the moments of celebration and the times of quiet endurance. You have never abandoned me, never overlooked me, and never failed to sustain me. As I look back, I see Your faithfulness woven into every chapter of my story. Lord, teach me to live with intentional remembrance. Let me not rush into new seasons without honoring what You have already done. Keep my heart anchored in gratitude and my spirit steady in praise. May Thanksgiving guard me from forgetfulness, and may worship continually rise from my lips as acknowledgment of Your goodness. Today, I decree and declare that I remember the Lord with praise and thanksgiving. Joy fills my seasons, transitions, and new beginnings. My worship rises as a memorial before God. Divine favor rests upon my days and decisions. Gratitude anchors my heart in every circumstance. I will not forget His benefits, I will not overlook His mercy, and I will not take His faithfulness for granted. As I step into new seasons, I do so with joy, confidence, and holy expectation. The same God who sustained me yesterday goes before me tomorrow. I trust Your guidance, rest in Your presence, and lift my voice in continual praise. In Jesus mighty name, Amen.

SCRIPTURE READING

Numbers 23:23 "Surely there is no enchantment against Jacob, neither is there any divination against Israel: according to this time it shall be said of Jacob and of Israel, What hath God wrought!"

REFLECTION AND ENCOURAGEMENT

This verse is a powerful proclamation of divine authority, covenant protection, and irreversible victory. It establishes a spiritual truth that cannot be contested: no force of darkness, no hidden manipulation, and no spoken curse has power over what God has blessed. Enchantments and divinations represent unseen strategies attempting to interfere, manipulate outcomes, or derail destiny through spiritual or emotional opposition. Yet God declares that none of these can prevail against His people. When God places His covenant upon a life, every opposing force is rendered powerless. What is covered by God cannot be reversed by man or darkness. This passage reminds us that outcomes are not determined by attacks, but by God's word. Opposition may arise, but it does not get the final say. God's authority overrides every scheme, and His purpose stands firm regardless of resistance. The verse also points us toward testimony. There comes a moment, according to this time, when God's intervention becomes visible and undeniable. What once appeared threatened, delayed, or uncertain will become clear evidence of God's power. Your life will speak louder than opposition, declaring not what the enemy tried to do, but what God has done. Stand confidently in this truth: you are not exposed or vulnerable. Your life is governed by divine authority. And in due time, it will be said concerning you, "What hath God wrought!"

DIVINELY GUARDED AND GUARANTEED!

PRAYER AND DAILY DECLARATION

HEAVENLY Father, I thank You for Your everlasting covenant and supreme authority over my life. You are the Sovereign Lord, and no power in heaven, on earth, or beneath the earth can override what You have spoken. I stand under the covering of Your covenant, secured by the blood of Jesus and upheld by Your unchanging Word. Lord, I acknowledge that every battle I face is subject to Your authority. Every unseen force, every whispered accusation, every hidden scheme is exposed and rendered powerless under Your name. You are my shield and my strong defense. I will not fear opposition, for greater is He who is in me than any force against me. Today, I decree and declare that no enchantment, divination, or hidden scheme can prevail against me. Every assignment of darkness is dismantled; every curse is reversed, every plan formed against my destiny is nullified. God's covenant stands as my defense and my victory. I stand clothed in divine authority, I walk backed by heaven, and I move under the power of the Holy Spirit. Every voice that rises against what God has spoken over me is silenced. Every attempt to delay, derail, or diminish my destiny is overturned. What God has blessed cannot be cursed. What He has ordained cannot be stopped. I declare victory over my life, my household, and my future. I advance in boldness, knowing that the Lord of Hosts fights for me. My life will continually testify to God's power, faithfulness, and triumph. In Jesus mighty name, Amen.

SCRIPTURE READING

REFLECTION AND ENCOURAGEMENT

This verse powerfully illustrates the authority and urgency of God's voice. When a lion roars, it commands attention. Everything within hearing range responds instinctively. In the same way, when God speaks, His word carries weight, direction, and divine authority that calls for a response. God's voice is not casual or uncertain. When He speaks, it awakens purpose, stirs courage, and calls alignment. His word does not leave you passive; it invites movement. The question in this verse is not whether God has spoken, but how His people will respond. Silence is not neutrality when God has released instruction; obedience becomes the natural response of a listening heart. This passage also teaches that boldness is born from obedience, not personality. When God speaks, He releases the grace to respond. Fear does not come from His voice; confidence does. As you stay attentive to Him, hesitation gives way to courage, and clarity replaces doubt. God never demands obedience without also supplying strength. To prophesy here is not limited to speaking aloud; it represents acting in alignment with what God has revealed. It is living out His instruction, moving when He says move, and standing firm when He says stand. When God has spoken, obedience becomes both a privilege and a calling. So do not shrink back. God's voice equips you to rise. When He speaks, He is inviting you into purpose, movement, and divine partnership. Respond boldly. His words carry everything you need to obey.

LISTEN, RISE, OBEY!

PRAYER AND DAILY DECLARATION

HEAVENLY Father, I thank You for speaking into my life with clarity and kindness. Your voice is steady, gentle, and trustworthy. You do not lead me with confusion, but with peace. I quiet my heart before You and choose to listen with humility and trust. Lord, soften anything in me that resists Your instruction. Remove haste, fear, and distraction. Teach me to recognize Your voice above every other voice. Let my spirit remain tender and responsive to Your leading. When You speak, give me the grace to obey without striving and the courage to move without hesitation. Today, I decree and declare that my heart is attentive to the voice of God. I am not rushed; I am led. Fear does not control my response. Grace empowers my obedience. Peace confirms my direction. I choose surrender over self-will, I choose trust over uncertainty. I choose obedience rooted in love. Align my life fully with Your calling and purpose. Shape my responses to reflect faith, maturity, and quiet confidence. When You speak, I will rise gently, respond faithfully, and walk steadily in what You have declared. I rest in the assurance that Your guidance is good, Your timing is perfect, and Your presence is with me always. In Jesus mighty name, Amen.

SCRIPTURE READING

REFLECTION AND ENCOURAGEMENT

This verse is a firm and comforting declaration of God's absolute authority. It reminds you that no plan, threat, report, or intention, no matter how loud or intimidating, can succeed unless God permits it. When the Lord speaks, His word settles the matter completely. Isaiah 7:7 reveals an important truth: not everything spoken against you is sanctioned by heaven. Situations may appear urgent, powerful, or convincing, but God alone determines what stands and what collapses. When God declares, "It shall not stand," He is canceling outcomes before they ever manifest. This word releases peace. God does not ask you to fight every battle or argue every accusation. He invites you to rest in His sovereignty. What He has disallowed cannot resurrect itself, regroup, or overpower His will. His authority silences fear and dismantles opposition at the root. This passage reassures you that God is actively guarding your future. His word overrides unstable circumstances and contradicting voices. You are not at the mercy of reports you are anchored in God's declaration. What He nullifies is finished, and what He establishes is secure.

RESTING IN HIS WORD!

PRAYER AND DAILY DECLARATION

HEAVENLY Father, I thank You for being sovereign, faithful, and completely unshaken by opposition. Nothing surprises You, nothing intimidates You, and nothing overturns what You have spoken. You reign above every circumstance, every report, and every unseen force. Because You are secure, I am secure. Lord, I choose to trust Your Word above every fear, every negative voice, and every conflicting report. When uncertainty tries to rise, anchor me in truth. When pressure attempts to overwhelm me, steady my heart with peace. Teach me to measure every situation against what You have declared, not the other way around. Today, I decree and declare that every plan not ordained by God will not stand. God's word overrides every negative report. Fear has no authority over my heart or mind; peace guards my spirit and steadies my steps. God's purpose prevails fully in my life. I will not be moved by what I see, I will not be shaken by what I hear, I will remain grounded in what You have spoken. I rest in Your authority and receive the assurance that Your Word is final. What You have promised cannot be undone. What You have established cannot be reversed. Let Your peace rule my heart and Your truth govern my future. I walk forward confident, calm, and anchored in the certainty that Your purposes will stand. In Jesus mighty name, Amen.

SCRIPTURE READING

REFLECTION AND ENCOURAGEMENT

This verse reveals God's intentional design for wholeness, continuity, and completion in your life. It speaks directly against loss, interruption, barrenness, and premature endings. God declares stability over your body, your purpose, and every work committed into your hands. God's promise here is comprehensive. He does not merely address fruitfulness. He addresses preservation. Nothing is cut short, nothing is wasted, and nothing is aborted under His care. The fulfillment of your days means your life unfolds according to divine order, not fear, sickness, or limitation. This passage also reminds you that fruitfulness is covenant-based, not accidental. God Himself sustains life, productivity, and strength. Whether in your body, your calling, your family, or your assignment, God declares increase, continuity, and completion. You are not living under cycles of loss or depletion. God is committed to finishing what He has started in you. Your days are filled with purpose, your strength is renewed, and your life reflects the faithfulness of a God who fulfills His promises fully.

FULLNESS OF DAYS!

PRAYER AND DAILY DECLARATION

HEAVENLY Father, I thank You for Your promise of wholeness, fruitfulness, and divine health. You are intentional with my life, and nothing You have ordained for me will be incomplete or unfulfilled. I receive Your covering over my body, my work, my calling, and every area entrusted to me. You are the keeper of my strength and the sustainer of my purpose. Lord, where weakness attempts to arise, release renewal. Where delay has tried to discourage me, establish steady growth, let my life reflect the evidence of Your preserving hand. Guard my health, strengthen my labor, and bless the work of my hands so that it produces lasting fruit. Today, I decree and declare that nothing in my life is barren, wasted, or cut short. God strengthens my body, my purpose, and my labor. My days are fulfilled according to God's perfect will. Fruitfulness flows in every season of my life. Divine health and stability are established within me. I am not diminished, I am sustained. I am not depleted, I am renewed. I am not unfinished, I am upheld by covenant promise. I rest in Your faithfulness, trusting that You preserve my life, sustain my strength, and complete every purpose You have ordained. Let my life unfold in fullness, alignment, and steady blessing, according to Your wisdom and grace. In Jesus mighty name, Amen.

SCRIPTURE READING

Exodus 14:15 "Speak unto the children of Israel, that they go forward."

REFLECTION AND ENCOURAGEMENT

This verse is a decisive call to faith-filled action. Israel stood at the edge of the Red Sea with obstacles before them and pressure behind them, yet God's instruction was not to remain still, but to move forward. This reminds us that God often calls progress before the path becomes visible. Faith is not waiting for certainty; it is trusting God enough to step when He speaks. God had already prepared the miracle before Israel took a single step. The sea did not part; first obedience came first. This teaches us that divine breakthroughs are often activated by movement. While prayer aligns the heart, obedience engages the hand of God. Remaining still may feel safe, but it allows fear to linger. Moving forward, even when unsure, releases faith and invites God's power into action. This passage also reassures us that God never commands movement without provision. He goes ahead of His people, making a way where none seems possible. The instruction to go forward is evidence that God is already at work beyond what you can see. What appears blocked is not final. God specializes in opening paths through impossibilities. So take courage. Forward movement is an act of trust and surrender. As you obey, God reveals the way step by step. You do not need to see the entire journey, only to take the next step in faith. When God says go forward, the victory is already in motion.

OBEDIENCE ACTIVATES THE WAY FORWARD!

PRAYER AND DAILY DECLARATION

HEAVENLY Father, I thank You for calling me forward in faith. You do not call me to remain where I was, but to grow, to advance, and to trust You beyond what I can see. Even when the path is not fully clear, You are already there. You go before me, preparing what I cannot yet perceive and aligning what I cannot yet understand. Lord, I choose obedience over fear. When hesitation rises, strengthen my resolve. When uncertainty whispers, steady my heart. Teach me to step forward with quiet confidence, knowing that Your presence is greater than any unknown. I will not allow fear to define my pace or limit my progress. Today, I decree and declare that I move forward in faith, fear no longer holds me back, and God makes a way before me. Obstacles give way to God's power, victory unfolds as I obey. My steps are ordered by the Lord, my path is prepared ahead of me. I am surrounded and supported on every side. I trust You to guide my steps, part every barrier, and open doors no one can shut. I move forward with confidence, not because I see the whole journey, but because I trust the One who leads me. I advance in peace, strengthened by faith and upheld by Your faithful hand. In Jesus mighty name, Amen.

SCRIPTURE READING

REFLECTION AND ENCOURAGEMENT

These verses offer a deeply comforting revelation of God's tender compassion toward human frailty. God is not distant from your weakness. He understands it completely. He knows your limits, your strength, and the moments when you feel overwhelmed. Rather than responding with disappointment, He meets you with mercy, patience, and care. God remembers that you are dust. This does not diminish your value; it magnifies His compassion. He does not expect you to carry life's weight by sheer strength or perfection. He acknowledges your humanity and responds with grace that sustains you where your strength falls short. While human life is fragile and fleeting like grass, God's care is steady and enduring. Circumstances may change, seasons may pass, and strength may fluctuate, but His compassion does not fade. Where human ability is temporary, God's faithfulness remains constant. This passage reassures you that you are upheld not by your capacity to endure, but by God's covenant love. You are gently carried through every season, carefully guarded in moments of weakness, and deeply known by a God who remembers you with mercy. You are safe in His care, even when you feel fragile.

SUSTAINED BY MERCY AND GRACE!

PRAYER AND DAILY DECLARATION

HEAVENLY Father, I thank You that You know me completely and love me deeply. Nothing about me is hidden from You, not my strengths, not my struggles, not my silent battles. Yet You meet me not with judgment, but with compassion. In every season of my life, You remain patient, attentive, and kind. Lord, when I feel aware of my limitations, remind me that Your grace is sufficient. When I feel weary, draw me closer instead of letting me pull away. You do not demand perfection from me You offer presence. You do not withdraw when I am weak. You sustain me in it. Today, I decree and declare that I rest in the mercy of the Lord. God's compassion sustains my life. My weakness is covered by His grace; I am upheld by God's faithful care. I am gently guided and preserved by the Lord. I release the burden of self-reliance, I release the pressure to carry what You have already taken, I receive Your sustaining grace. Carry me where I am weak. Strengthen me where I am weary. Guard my heart from striving and anchor me in trust. Let me live from a place of being loved, upheld, and gently led by You. I choose to rest in the assurance that Your compassion never fails and Your care never wavers. In Jesus mighty name, Amen.

SCRIPTURE READING

REFLECTION AND ENCOURAGEMENT

This verse reveals one of the most comforting truths about God's character: He moves with intention and timing. Mercy is not random. Favor is not accidental. There is a "set time" appointed by God for restoration, breakthrough, and divine intervention. When seasons feel prolonged, or prayers seem delayed, it is easy to assume that God is distant. Yet this scripture reminds you that God rises at the appointed time. He is never late. He is never rushed. He acts precisely when His purpose and timing align. The phrase "the set time" speaks of divine appointment. What is scheduled in heaven cannot be canceled by earthly delay. God sees the full picture. He understands the preparation required before favor manifests. What feels like waiting may be positioning. Mercy precedes favor. Before God restores publicly, He strengthens privately. Before elevation, there is refinement. Before breakthrough, there is preparation. When the set time arrives, what seemed dormant begins to rise. You are not forgotten in delay. You are being prepared for appointed favor. When God arises on your behalf, circumstances shift, doors open, and restoration unfolds according to His perfect plan.

THE SET TIME
OF FAVOR HAS COME!

PRAYER AND DAILY DECLARATION

HEAVENLY Father, I thank You that You are a God of mercy, precision, and divine timing. You are never early and never late. You rise at the appointed moment, and Your plans unfold exactly as You have ordained. When my heart feels weary from waiting, I remind myself that heaven operates on a set time that cannot be altered by human limitation. Today, I decree and declare with confidence that God appoints the set time of favor over my life. Mercy speaks over me. Delay does not define me. What You have scheduled in heaven cannot be canceled on earth. I decree that divine favor is unfolding in due season. Doors that were closed are opening according to Your timing. Restoration is not random; it is ordained. Breakthrough is not accidental; it is appointed. I declare that I will not grow discouraged in seasons of preparation. God is arising on my behalf. Circumstances are aligning. Divine opportunities are being positioned in the proper order. The mercy of God surrounds my present, and the favor of God governs my future. I trust Your timing. I rest in Your faithfulness. I walk forward with expectancy, knowing that when You arise, nothing can resist Your will. In Jesus mighty name. Amen.

SCRIPTURE READING

Psalm 107:2 "Let the redeemed of the LORD say so, whom he hath redeemed from the hand of the enemy."

REFLECTION AND ENCOURAGEMENT

This verse is both an invitation and a command. Redemption is not meant to be silent. Those whom the Lord has delivered are called to testify. To be redeemed means you were rescued, restored, and brought out of what once held you captive. It is evidence of God's mercy in motion. Redemption is personal. It speaks of battles won, chains broken, fears overcome, and seasons survived. God does not redeem quietly; He redeems powerfully. When you declare what He has done, you strengthen your faith and encourage others who are still waiting for their breakthrough. Silence can sometimes minimize what God has accomplished. But testimony magnifies His faithfulness. When you "say so," you remind yourself that you are no longer defined by past struggles or former bondage. You are marked by deliverance. Your story carries weight. The hand of the enemy did not prevail. God intervened. He restored. He redeemed. Speaking that truth reinforces your identity and glorifies His power. You are not who you used to be. You are redeemed.

I AM REDEEMED AND I WILL TESTIFY!

PRAYER AND DAILY DECLARATION

HEAVENLY Father, I thank You for redeeming my life from the hand of the enemy. You did not overlook my struggle or abandon me in my weakness. You stepped into my story with mercy and power. You rescued me from fear that tried to paralyze me, from bondage that tried to confine me, from sin that tried to define me, and from every scheme meant to destroy my purpose. Lord, I acknowledge that my freedom is not self-earned but divinely given. It is the gift of Your grace, the evidence of Your covenant love, and the result of Christ's finished work. What You have done for me is sacred, powerful, and worthy of remembrance. Give me the courage to testify to Your goodness. Remove hesitation, insecurity, or fear that tries to silence my voice. Let my words carry gratitude and truth. Remind me continually of where You brought me from and how faithfully You carried me through every valley. Today, I decree and declare that I am redeemed by the Lord. The enemy does not define my story; God's mercy defines me. My past does not control my future; deliverance marks my life. I will speak of His faithfulness, I will remember His saving power, and I will not minimize what He has done for me. My testimony strengthens my faith and encourages others. What once tried to defeat me now magnifies God's power. What once caused pain now reveals His grace. My life stands as evidence that God rescues, restores, and redeems completely. I stand redeemed, restored, and victorious in Christ, not ashamed, not silenced, but grateful and bold. In Jesus mighty name, Amen.

SCRIPTURE READING

Psalm 103:17–18 "But the mercy of the LORD is from everlasting to everlasting upon them that fear him, and his righteousness unto children's children; To such as keep his covenant, and to those that remember his commandments to do them."

REFLECTION AND ENCOURAGEMENT

These verses beautifully extend the promise of God's compassion into eternity. While human life is fragile and fleeting, God's mercy is unchanging, continuous, and everlasting. His love does not expire with seasons, strength, or circumstance it endures beyond time itself. God's mercy is not momentary kindness; it is covenant love. It rests upon those who walk with Him, trust Him, and remember Him. Even when life feels uncertain or strength feels limited, His mercy remains firmly in place. You are not sustained by consistency in perfection, but by faithfulness in relationship. This passage also speaks of legacy. God's righteousness reaches beyond you to your children and generations yet to come. What He establishes in your life does not end with you. Your obedience, faith, and trust become seeds of blessing that outlive your present moment. These verses remind you that you are anchored in something eternal. God's care stretches backward and forward, covering your past, sustaining your present, and securing your future. You are held by a mercy that cannot be exhausted and a righteousness that will not fail.

EVER-ENDURING

MERCY

PRAYER AND DAILY DECLARATION

HEAVENLY Father, I thank You for Your everlasting mercy and covenant love that surrounds my life. Your compassion is not seasonal or conditional; it is steadfast and enduring. It does not waver with my weakness, nor does it fade with time. From generation to generation, You remain faithful, and I am covered by that unbreakable promise. Lord, I rest in the security of Your covenant. When I feel uncertain, remind me that Your mercy is already ahead of me. When I reflect on my past, I see Your hand preserving me. When I look toward the future, I trust that Your faithfulness will sustain me. Your love is not fragile; it is firm and eternal. Today, I decree and declare that the mercy of the Lord rests upon my life. God's covenant love sustains me daily. Righteousness flows through my generations, my obedience produces lasting fruit, and my life is anchored in God's eternal care. I am not drifting; I am established in covenant. I am not forgotten; I am remembered by mercy. I am not uncertain, I am upheld by promise. Let my life reflect Your faithfulness in every season. May my choices today create a legacy of righteousness tomorrow. Let Your mercy extend through me to my household, to my community, and to generations yet unborn. I trust You with my present and my future, confident that the same covenant love that carried me this far will carry me all the way. In Jesus mighty name, Amen.

SCRIPTURE READING

REFLECTION AND ENCOURAGEMENT

This verse offers deep reassurance for every season of uncertainty, pressure, or distress. God is not distant when trouble arises. He is very present. His help is not delayed, conditional, or uncertain. It is immediate, intentional, and reliable. To call God a refuge means He is a safe place you can run to without fear. A refuge is not merely protection from danger; it is shelter, rest, and security. When life feels overwhelming, God does not stand on the sidelines. He becomes your hiding place. God is also described as strong. This means He does not only shield you from difficulty; He empowers you to endure it. When your strength feels depleted, His strength becomes available. You are not expected to carry the weight alone. God supplies what you lack. This passage reminds you that trouble does not signal abandonment. It often becomes the place where God's nearness is most clearly revealed. You are not unsupported, unseen, or forgotten. God is present, powerful, and actively involved in helping you through.

STRENGTH IN

STILLNESS!

PRAYER AND DAILY DECLARATION

HEAVENLY Father, I thank You for being my refuge and my strength. You are not distant in difficulty, nor silent in struggle. In times of trouble, You are present and attentive to my cry, aware of my burden, and ready to help. You are my shelter when storms arise and my stability when everything feels uncertain. Lord, when situations feel heavy or unclear, remind me that I can run to You without hesitation or fear. When my strength feels diminished, teach me to lean fully into Yours. Where I am tempted to strive in my own ability, draw me back into rest. Let Your presence calm what tries to overwhelm me and steady what tries to shake me. Today, I decree and declare that God is my refuge and safe place. God's strength upholds me; His divine help is present in my situation. I am not overwhelmed; I am not abandoned. I am supported by God's unfailing care, I am surrounded by His sustaining grace, and I am guided by His faithful hand. I place every concern, burden, and challenge into Your hands. I release what I cannot control and receive the peace that comes from trusting You. Sustain me when I feel weak. Strengthen me when I feel uncertain. Guide me through each moment with clarity and confidence. I rest in the assurance that my refuge is secure and my help is near. In Jesus mighty name, Amen.

SCRIPTURE READING

Hebrews 4:16 "Let us therefore come boldly unto the throne of grace, that we may obtain mercy, and find grace to help in time of need."

REFLECTION AND ENCOURAGEMENT

This verse is a gracious invitation from God, not a command rooted in fear, but an open door framed by love. God does not ask you to approach Him timidly, ashamed, or uncertain of your place. Through Christ, you are welcomed fully and confidently into His presence. The throne you approach is not one of condemnation or judgment; it is a throne of grace. Grace means you are received not because you earned it, but because God delights in extending mercy. When life feels overwhelming, when answers are unclear, and when strength feels low, God does not withdraw. He invites you closer. Boldness here is not arrogance; it is assurance. It is known that your access to God is secured by Christ, not by your performance. In moments of weakness, confusion, or need, you are not turned away. Instead, you are met with mercy for the past and grace for the present moment. This passage reminds you that help is never delayed or distant. Grace is available exactly when you need it most. You are never an inconvenience to God. Every time you come to Him, you are received with compassion, understanding, and divine support.

THE THRONE OF GRACE
IS ALWAYS OPEN!

PRAYER AND DAILY DECLARATION

HEAVENLY Father, I thank You for the open invitation to come boldly into Your presence. Through Christ, I am not kept at a distance; I am welcomed with confidence, peace, and acceptance. Your throne is not a place of condemnation, but a place of grace. It is where mercy flows freely, and help is abundantly supplied. Lord, when I feel weak, uncertain, or in need, I remind myself that access to You is never restricted. I do not have to prove myself worthy to come before You. I do not have to hide my struggles or mask my need. You already know, and You still invite me closer. Teach me to approach You without hesitation and without fear. Today, I lay down every burden of self-doubt, shame, or striving. I release the pressure to carry what only You can hold. I receive Your mercy afresh and allow Your grace to meet me right where I am. Today, I decree and declare that I approach God with confidence and faith. Mercy is released over my life, and Grace meets me in my time of need. Divine help is available to me now. I am strengthened, supported, and upheld by God. I am not rejected, I am received, I am not alone, I am welcomed. I am not without help; I am supplied with grace. I receive Your grace for today and trust You for everything ahead. I rest in the assurance that Your help is timely, sufficient, and constant. Your presence is my covering, and Your mercy is my confidence. In Jesus mighty name, Amen.

SCRIPTURE READING

Psalm 91:16 "With long life will I satisfy him, and shew him my salvation."

REFLECTION AND ENCOURAGEMENT

This verse is a deeply personal promise from God, one that speaks not only of length of days, but of the quality and purpose of those days. God's desire is not merely that you live long, but that your life be filled, satisfying, and anchored in His saving power. To be satisfied with God means to live with a settled heart. It is the assurance that your life is not slipping through your fingers without meaning. God promises a life marked by fulfillment where peace replaces anxiety, purpose replaces confusion, and trust replaces fear. Satisfaction here is not dependent on circumstance; it flows from living under God's covering. God also promises to show you His salvation. This means His deliverance is not hidden or distant. He reveals His saving hand again and again through protection, healing, restoration, and timely rescue. Each season becomes an opportunity to witness His faithfulness at work in your life. This reflection invites you to rest in God's long-term care. Your future is not uncertain or unguarded. Your days are held in God's hands, preserved by His promise, and shaped by His loving intention. You are living a life that God Himself is committed to sustaining.

SATISFIED IN HIM!

PRAYER AND DAILY DECLARATION

HEAVENLY Father, I thank You for Your promise of long life, fulfillment, and salvation. My days are not accidental or fragile in Your hands; they are intentionally preserved and purposefully ordered. You hold my timeline, and You govern my future with wisdom and care. Nothing about my life is left to chance. Lord, teach me to live each day with gratitude and trust. Help me to see beyond the moment and recognize that You are shaping my story with intention. When I reflect on the past, I see Your preserving hand. When I look at the present, I sense Your sustaining grace. When I consider the future, I rest in Your faithful promise. Reveal Your saving power to me in every season through protection when I do not see danger, through provision when needs arise, through healing when strength feels diminished, and through deliverance when obstacles appear. Let me recognize Your hand at work in ways both visible and invisible. Today, I decree and declare that God preserves my life, and my days are filled with purpose and peace. I walk in divine satisfaction, not emptiness. God continually reveals His salvation to me. My future is secure in the hands of the Lord. I am not cut short, I am sustained. I am not wandering, I am guided. I am not unfulfilled; I am satisfied in Him. I receive Your promise with faith and quiet confidence. I rest in the assurance that my life is covered, guided, and brought to completion according to Your perfect will. In Jesus mighty name, Amen.

SCRIPTURE READING

Ephesians 6:18 "Praying always with all prayer and supplication in the Spirit, and watching thereunto with all perseverance and supplication for all saints;

REFLECTION AND ENCOURAGEMENT

This verse reveals that prayer is not occasional; it is continual. Apostle Paul places prayer at the end of the armor of God passage, showing that spiritual strength is sustained through ongoing communion with the Lord. Prayer is not simply a moment of asking; it is a posture of dependence. To pray "always" does not mean nonstop words, but a consistent awareness of God's presence and guidance. It means your heart remains connected, responsive, and aligned. Prayer becomes the atmosphere in which you live. The phrase "with all perseverance" reminds you that prayer requires endurance. There will be seasons when answers are delayed, when circumstances seem unchanged, and when fatigue tempts you to stop. Yet perseverance in prayer builds spiritual resilience. It keeps your heart steady and your focus fixed on God. This verse also widens your perspective. Prayer is not only for personal needs but also for others. Intercession strengthens the body of Christ. As you pray for fellow believers, unity grows and spiritual strength multiplies. Prayer is your lifeline. It keeps you alert, aligned, and spiritually equipped.

ANCHORED THROUGH PRAYER!

PRAYER AND DAILY DECLARATION

HEAVENLY Father, teach me to live in continual communion with You. Let prayer become more than practice, let it become the rhythm of my life and the posture of my heart. May I not turn to You only in moments of crisis but walk with You in steady dependence each day. Shape my thoughts through conversation with You. Anchor my decisions in time spent before You. Keep my spirit attentive to Your voice and my heart sensitive to Your correction and guidance. Remove distraction, dullness, and spiritual complacency. Let me remain watchful, discerning, and aligned with heaven's purposes. When answers seem delayed or circumstances remain unchanged, strengthen me to persevere without losing hope. Teach me that waiting in prayer is never wasted. Today, I decree and declare with confidence that I remain steadfast in prayer, I am spiritually alert, and aligned with God's will, and I will not grow weary or distracted. My prayers rise before You with faith and humility, and I intercede with compassion and conviction. Prayer sustains my faith, prayer sharpens my discernment, prayer fortifies my spirit against spiritual attack. Through prayer, I remain anchored when life feels uncertain, equipped when challenges arise, and strengthened when pressure increases. I trust that You hear me, that You respond with wisdom, and that Your purposes are unfolding even when unseen. Let my life be marked by consistent communion, steady trust, and unwavering devotion. In Jesus mighty name, Amen.

SCRIPTURE READING

Psalm 118:17 "I shall not die, but live, and declare the works of the LORD."

REFLECTION AND ENCOURAGEMENT

This verse is a bold declaration of life spoken in the face of opposition. It is not merely a hopeful statement; it is a confession rooted in confidence in God's preserving power. The psalmist declares life not as a possibility, but as a divine certainty anchored in God's purpose. To say "I shall live" is to acknowledge that your life is intentionally sustained by God. You are preserved not just to exist, but to declare, testify, and bear witness to the works of the Lord. Every breath you take carries an assignment. Every season you survive carries testimony. This passage reminds you that God is the author of your days. Your life is not at the mercy of circumstances, fear, or opposition. When God preserves you, it is because there is still purpose to be fulfilled and glory to be revealed through your life. Even when challenges arise, this verse calls you to speak life over yourself. It encourages you to reject premature endings and embrace God's promise of continuation. Your story is still unfolding, and God is not finished with you yet.

I SHALL LIVE
AND TESTIFY!

PRAYER AND DAILY DECLARATION

HEAVENLY Father, I thank You for the gift of life and for the purpose You have intentionally attached to it. My existence is not accidental, and my days are not random. They are held in Your hands, measured, preserved, and directed by Your wisdom. You are the One who sustains my breath and orders my steps. When fear tries to whisper against my future, remind me that Your Word speaks life over me. When uncertainty attempts to cloud my vision, anchor me in the truth that I am preserved for purpose and protected for testimony. Strengthen my faith to stand firm in what You have declared, even when circumstances try to suggest otherwise. Today, I decree and declare that I shall live and not die. My life is preserved by God's hand; no premature end will interrupt my purpose, and my days are filled with divine intention. I will declare the works of the Lord; I am sustained by covenant promise, I am guarded by divine authority, and I am established for lasting impact. Let my life bring glory to You in every season. May my testimony reflect Your preserving grace and faithful guidance. I rise today with confidence, gratitude, and assurance, knowing that You who began a good work in me will bring it to completion. I move forward aware that my life is valuable, purposeful, and securely held in Your care. In Jesus mighty name, Amen.

SCRIPTURE READING

REFLECTION AND ENCOURAGEMENT

This verse is an invitation to allow God's Word to take up deep and lasting residence within you, not as a passing thought or occasional reference, but as a living presence that shapes how you think, speak, respond, and worship. To let the Word of Christ dwell richly means to give it room to influence every area of your life. When God's Word dwells richly within you, it becomes a source of wisdom and stability. It anchors you when emotions fluctuate and guides you when decisions feel unclear. The Word does not merely inform you, it transforms you from the inside out, aligning your heart with God's truth and your actions with His will. This passage also reveals that God's Word naturally produces worship. When truth settles deeply in your heart, praise flows freely from your lips. Worship becomes more than a song; it becomes a lifestyle expressed through gratitude, obedience, and grace-filled living. As you allow God's Word to dwell richly within you, your life becomes a vessel of encouragement to others. Wisdom flows through your speech, grace seasons your interactions, and worship rises naturally from a heart rooted in truth. You become both strengthened, fed by the Word, and equipped to nourish others.

LET GOD'S WORD
DWELL WITHIN!

PRAYER AND DAILY DECLARATION

HEAVENLY Father, I thank You for Your living and powerful Word. Your Word is not distant, outdated, or empty; it is alive, active, and able to discern the thoughts and intentions of my heart. It carries authority to shape me, correct me, strengthen me, and establish me in truth. Lord, I open myself fully to receive Your Word not casually or superficially, but deeply and richly. Create in me a hunger for Scripture and a desire to meditate on it daily. Let Your Word take root within me, transforming the way I think, speak, and respond. Where confusion has existed, bring clarity. Where fear has lingered, replace it with truth. Where weakness has shown, release strength through Your promises. Teach me to make room for Your Word in my thoughts and in my decisions. Let it become my foundation when emotions shift and circumstances change. Let it guard my heart, steady my spirit, and align my life with heaven's perspective. Today, I decree and declare that the Word of Christ dwells richly within me, and God's truth renews my mind. Wisdom and grace flow from my life, my heart overflows with worship and gratitude, and my life reflects God's truth and glory. Your Word anchors me, Your Word corrects me, Your Word empowers me. Let my words encourage, my actions honor You, and my heart remain steadfast in Your promises. I live today strengthened by truth, guided by wisdom, and filled with grace that flows from Your living Word. In Jesus mighty name, Amen.

SCRIPTURE READING

REFLECTION AND ENCOURAGEMENT

This commandment is unique because it carries a promise attached to it. God connects honor with longevity, stability, and blessing, revealing that the posture of your heart can influence the course of your life. Honor is not merely an action; it is an attitude rooted in humility, respect, and obedience. To honor those God has placed in your life is to recognize divine order. It does not require perfection from people; it requires alignment with God's instruction. Even when relationships are complex or imperfect, choosing honor positions your heart to walk in wisdom and peace. Honor creates space for God's blessing to flow. It fosters stability in your journey and guards your steps from unnecessary turmoil. When you choose honor, you are choosing a path that invites God's covering, direction, and favor. This verse reminds you that obedience is not restrictive; it is protective. God's instructions are given in love, designed to preserve you and guide you into a life marked by peace, longevity, and divine order.

HONOR UNLOCKS BLESSINGS!

PRAYER AND DAILY DECLARATION

HEAVENLY Father, I thank You for Your wisdom and loving instruction. Your commands are not burdensome; they are protective, purposeful, and rooted in covenant love. Everything You ask of me is designed to preserve my life, strengthen my character, and align me with blessings. Teach my heart to walk in honor, humility, and willing obedience before You. Let obedience flow from love, not pressure. Shape my posture so that reverence for You governs my words, attitudes, and actions. Where dishonor, resentment, pride, or misunderstanding have taken root, bring healing. Replace them with grace, patience, and understanding. Help me to honor those You have placed in my life not merely from duty, but from a heart aligned with Your order and wisdom. Let my relationships reflect maturity, stability, and peace. Today, I decree and declare that my heart walks in honor. I choose humility and obedience. God's blessing rests upon my life. My days are marked by peace and longevity; my path is stable and ordered by God. Obedience positions me for promise. Honor opens the door to peace, and humility strengthens my foundation. I receive the promise attached to obedience and trust that my life is preserved and blessed as I walk in Your ways. Establish me in righteousness, secure my future, and let my obedience produce generational fruit. In Jesus mighty name, Amen.

SCRIPTURE READING

REFLECTION AND ENCOURAGEMENT

This passage lovingly redirects the heart from anxiety to assurance. God does not deny the reality of pressure, concern, or uncertainty, but He invites you to respond differently. Instead of carrying the weight alone, you are invited to rejoice, pray, and trust. Rejoicing here is not rooted in perfect circumstances; it is rooted in God's nearness. "The Lord is at hand" is a reminder that God is not distant or unaware. He is present, attentive, and actively involved in your life. His closeness is the foundation for peace. God gently instructs you not to be overwhelmed by worry, not because your concerns are insignificant, but because He is sufficient. Every anxious thought becomes an opportunity to pray. Every request becomes lighter when lifted with thanksgiving and trust. This passage teaches that peace flows from surrender. When you exchange worry for prayer and fear for gratitude, God's peace begins to guard your heart and mind. You are not called to live burdened; you are called to live anchored in trust, joy, and divine peace.

REJOICE, PRAY, AND
REST IN GOD'S PEACE!

PRAYER AND DAILY DECLARATION

HEAVENLY Father, I thank You for Your nearness and unwavering faithfulness. I choose to rejoice today not because everything around me feels settled, but because You are present, constant, and trustworthy. You see every detail of my life. Nothing is hidden from You, and nothing is outside Your care. Lord, I bring every concern, every unanswered question, and every lingering burden before You. I lay down the weight of overthinking, the pressure to control outcomes, and the fear of the unknown. Where anxiety has tried to settle in my heart, I replace it with prayer. Where worry has tried to take root, I choose thanksgiving. Where uncertainty has tried to shake me, I choose trust. Teach me to rest in Your peace rather than wrestle with worry. Let my heart be anchored in the assurance that You are near, not distant, not distracted, but attentive and involved. Guard my thoughts from spiraling and steady my emotions with Your presence. Today, I decree and declare that Joy fills my heart, and Anxiety has no hold over me. I trust God with every concern. Peace guards my heart and mind. The Lord is near and attentive to me. I am not consumed by worry; I am surrounded by peace. I am upheld by divine care. I rest in Your presence and walk forward with calm confidence, knowing that You are in control and Your peace surrounds me on every side. What I cannot resolve, You sustain. What I cannot see, You oversee. In Jesus mighty name, Amen.

SCRIPTURE READING

Exodus 3:21 "And I will give this people favour in the sight of the Egyptians: and it shall come to pass, that, when ye go, ye shall not go empty:"

REFLECTION AND ENCOURAGEMENT

This verse is a powerful promise that God does not allow seasons of hardship to end in loss. The children of Israel had endured years of oppression and labor, yet God declared that their exit would be marked by favor, restoration, and reward. What was taken from them would not remain unpaid. God is deeply aware of every season you have endured. He sees the sacrifices made, the tears shed, and the patience required to remain faithful in difficult times. Exodus 3:21 reminds you that God is intentional about restoration. He ensures that endurance is met with recompense and faithfulness with honor. Divine favor is not accidental; it is God actively shifting circumstances on your behalf. When God releases favor, doors open, hearts soften, and provision appears where it was once withheld. You are not leaving this season empty- handed; you are leaving with evidence of God's goodness. This passage encourages you to move forward with confidence. Your past struggle does not define your future outcome. God is restoring what was lost and adding reward to your obedience. Your exit is blessed, and your next season is marked by grace.

YOU WILL NOT LEAVE EMPTY-HANDED!

PRAYER AND DAILY DECLARATION

HEAVENLY Father, I thank You for seeing every season I have endured the quiet sacrifices, the unseen tears, the obedience when it was costly, and the trust when answers were delayed. Nothing about my perseverance has been overlooked. You are mindful of my faithfulness, and You remember every act of surrender offered in faith. Lord, I receive Your promise that I will not leave this season empty-handed. What was sown in tears will not be forgotten. What was endured in obedience will not go unrewarded. Release Your favor over my life in visible and tangible ways. Let restoration come where there was loss. Let strength return where there was weariness. Let honor replace hardship. I trust You to reward obedience and to bring beauty out of endurance. Where there was delay, let fulfillment arise. Where there was limitation, let expansion come. Where there was silence, let manifestation speak. Today, I decree and declare that God's favor surrounds me. I will not go empty-handed. Restoration is released into my life, my endurance is met with reward, and my next season is marked by grace and honor. What I carried in faith will produce fruit, what I endured in trust will produce testimony, what I surrendered in obedience will return in blessing. I move forward with confidence, knowing that You go before me, providing, restoring, and establishing every step. My season of faithfulness gives way to a season of fulfillment. In Jesus mighty name, Amen.

SCRIPTURE READING

Luke 2:52 "And Jesus increased in wisdom and stature, and in favor with God and man."

REFLECTION AND ENCOURAGEMENT

This verse gives us a beautiful picture of God's design for balanced, whole growth. Even Jesus, the Son of God, grew progressively. His growth was not rushed, forced, or one-dimensional. It unfolded naturally and intentionally, season by season, under the guidance of God. Luke 2:52 shows us that growth is meant to touch every area of life. Wisdom speaks to spiritual and mental development. Stature reflects physical strength and maturity. Favor with God and man reveals relational grace and divine approval. God's desire is not that you excel in one area while neglecting others, but that your life matures holistically. This passage also reassures you that growth is a process. You are not behind, deficient, or delayed. Where you are now is part of God's intentional unfolding. As you remain submitted to Him, He develops you steadily, adding wisdom, strengthening you inwardly and outwardly, and surrounding you with favor. Your life is not meant to be lopsided or strained. God leads you into balance, health, and grace. As you grow, He ensures that your increase is sustainable, your influence is healthy, and your favor is genuine and enduring.

MATURING IN WISDOM AND GRACE!

PRAYER AND DAILY DECLARATION

HEAVENLY Father, I thank You for Your intentional design for my growth and development. Nothing about my journey is random. Every season, every lesson, and every stretching moment is part of Your careful formation in my life. You are shaping me with purpose, refining my character, strengthening my foundation, and preparing me for what lies ahead. Lord, help me to grow in wisdom, strength, and grace. Guard my heart from comparison, impatience, or striving. When growth feels slow, remind me that roots are developing beneath the surface. When progress feels hidden, reassure me that transformation is still taking place. Teach me to trust Your timing and to embrace the process without frustration. Develop me fully spiritually grounded, mentally disciplined, physically strengthened, and relationally mature. Align every area of my life with Your will. Let my growth be balanced, steady, and sustained by Your Spirit rather than driven by pressure or performance. Today, I decree and declare that I increase in wisdom, I grow in strength and maturity, I walk in favor with God and with man. My life is balanced and well-ordered, and my growth is guided by God's Spirit. I am not stagnant, I am developing, I am not behind, I am being prepared, I am not overlooked, I am being formed. I embrace this season of development with gratitude and confidence. I trust You to complete the good work You have begun in me and to establish me fully in Your purpose. In Jesus mighty name, Amen.

SCRIPTURE READING

Nehemiah 2:6–9 "And the king said unto me, (the queen also sitting by him,) For how long shall thy journey be? and when wilt thou return? So it pleased the king to send me, and I set him a time… And the king granted me, according to the good hand of my God upon me… Moreover, I said unto the king, If it please the king, let letters be given me… And the king granted me… according to the good hand of my God upon me."

REFLECTION AND ENCOURAGEMENT

This passage reveals what happens when preparation meets prayer and prayer meets divine favor. Nehemiah did not rush into his assignment casually; he prayed, waited, planned, and trusted God. When the appointed moment arrived, God moved the heart of the king in his favor. Nehemiah's request was bold, yet it was backed by God's hand. Not only was permission granted, but provision and protection were released as well. Letters were issued, resources were supplied, and escorts were provided. This reminds us that when God authorizes an assignment, He also ensures support along the journey. This reflection reassures you that divine favor opens doors that human effort cannot force. When God's hand is upon you, resistance gives way, obstacles shift, and help appears in unexpected places. You are not stepping into your future; heaven is actively backing what God has assigned to you. Your role is obedience and trust. God's role is authorization, provision, and protection. When His good hand is upon your life, every step forward is sanctioned by heaven.

COMMISSIONED BY GOD, BACKED BY HEAVEN!

PRAYER AND DAILY DECLARATION

HEAVENLY Father, I thank You that Your good hand rests upon my life. Your favor is not accidental; it is intentional and covenant-based. You see every assignment You have placed in my heart, every vision You have stirred within me, and every step of obedience I have taken in faith. You are faithful to authorize what You initiate and to sustain what You call forth. As I move forward, grant me favor before the right people and alignment with the right opportunities. Open doors that no one can shut and close doors that are not ordained by You. Release provision, resources, partnerships, and protection for every step You have established. Where clarity is needed, provide direction. Where courage is required, strengthen my heart. Let me walk with confidence, not in my own ability, but in the assurance that I am supported by Your grace and upheld by Your authority. Guard me from striving and position me in divine timing. Today, I decree and declare the good hand of God is upon me, and divine doors open before me. Permission and provision are released. I move forward under heaven's authority. God goes ahead of me and makes the way clear. What God has approved cannot be hindered, what God has assigned will be accomplished, and what God has initiated will be sustained. I step forward with assurance, courage, and faith. I trust that You are clearing the path, ordering my steps, and establishing the work of my hands. In Jesus mighty name, Amen.

SCRIPTURE READING

1 Chronicles 4:10 "And Jabez called on the God of Israel, saying, Oh that thou wouldest bless me indeed, and enlarge my coast, and that thine hand might be with me, and that thou wouldest keep me from evil, that it may not grieve me! And God granted him that which he requested."

REFLECTION AND ENCOURAGEMENT

This verse reveals the beauty of bold, honest prayer. Jabez did not allow his past, his name, or his circumstances to define his future. Instead, he turned directly to God and asked for blessing, expansion, divine presence, and protection. His prayer was simple, sincere, and faith-filled, and God responded. Jabez teaches us that it is not wrong to ask God for more when "more" is aligned with purpose. God delights in blessing His children when their hearts are surrendered to Him. Expansion is not about pride or excess; it is about increased capacity to steward, influence, and serve according to God's will. The request for God's hand to be present reminds us that growth without God's presence becomes a burden, but growth with God's hand becomes grace. Jabez also understood the importance of protection, asking God to guard him from harm so that increase would not bring sorrow. This passage encourages you to pray boldly without apology. God is not intimidated by your requests. When your desires are rooted in faith and submission, God can bless you indeed and enlarge what He has placed in your care.

BLESSED, ENLARGED, AND KEPT BY GOD!

PRAYER AND DAILY DECLARATION

HEAVENLY Father, I come before You with a heart of trust and holy expectation. I thank You for being a God who hears sincere prayer and responds with compassion, wisdom, and power. You are attentive to my growth, my calling, and the assignments You have placed before me. I refuse to allow my past, my limitations, or my fears to restrict what You desire to do in my life. I release every mindset that keeps me small when You are calling me forward. I ask You to bless me indeed, not for selfish ambition, but for divine purpose. Enlarge my capacity so I can carry more responsibility with integrity. Expand my influence so that it reflects Your glory. Increase my wisdom so I can steward what You entrust to me faithfully. Let Your hand remain upon me, guiding, correcting, protecting, and establishing my steps. Keep me humble in growth and grounded in gratitude. Where You expand me, sustain me. Where You elevate me, mature me. Where You increase me, guard my heart. Today, I decree and declare that God blesses me indeed. My territory is enlarged by His hand. God's presence rests upon my life. I am kept from harm and sorrow. My increase is protected and purposeful. My expansion is aligned with heaven, My growth is sustained by grace, and my influence reflects God's goodness. I receive Your blessing with humility and thanksgiving. I trust You to expand my life in ways that glorify You, strengthen my character, and bring peace to my household and those connected to me. In Jesus mighty name, Amen.

SCRIPTURE READING

REFLECTION AND ENCOURAGEMENT

These verses carry the tender voice of God speaking directly to weary hearts. After seasons of struggle, discipline, and waiting, God does not come with rebuke. He comes with comfort. His words are deliberate, gentle, and restorative. He speaks peace where there has been pressure and reassurance where there has been fear. "Her warfare is accomplished" is a powerful declaration that struggle does not last forever. God sees the battles you have fought privately, the burdens you have carried quietly, and the endurance you have shown faithfully. This passage announces a turning point, the end of striving and the beginning of rest. God also declares pardon and restoration. He does not merely remove hardship; He heals the heart beneath it. Where guilt, shame, or heaviness once lingered, God speaks forgiveness and renewal. His comfort is not shallow; it reaches the deepest places of the soul. This reflection reminds you that God knows exactly when to bring relief. Your season of heaviness is not permanent. God Himself speaks comfort over you, signaling that restoration is unfolding and hope is being renewed.

YOUR WARFARE IS ENDED
REST IN GOD'S COMFORT!

PRAYER AND DAILY DECLARATION

HEAVENLY Father, I receive Your comfort today with humility and gratitude. You have seen every hidden battle, every silent tear, and every burden I have carried without complaint. Nothing about my endurance has gone unnoticed. You are gentle with my heart, patient with my process, and faithful in every season. Lord, You speak peace into places that have known strain and weariness. Where striving once marked my days, let rest now define them. Where conflict once surrounded me, let calm now settle. I release every weight of past struggle into Your hands, every disappointment, every misunderstanding, every prolonged season of pressure. Where warfare has exhausted me, I receive deep rest; where sorrow has lingered, I receive healing; where uncertainty has drained me, I receive steady hope. I trust that You are bringing my season of striving to a close. What once required constant defense now gives way to divine protection. What once demanded endurance now opens into restoration. Today, I decree and declare that God's comfort surrounds me. My warfare has come to an end. Restoration is unfolding in my life. Forgiveness and peace renew my heart. Hope is rising within me again. I am not defined by what I endured, I am strengthened by what You restored. I am not weary in spirit; I am refreshed by Your presence. I am not stepping into another battle; I am stepping into renewal. I rest in Your promises, confident that You are restoring my strength, reestablishing my joy, and renewing my future with peace. In Jesus mighty name, Amen.

SCRIPTURE READING

Psalm 70:4 "Let all those that seek thee rejoice and be glad in thee: and let such as love thy salvation say continually, Let God be magnified."

REFLECTION AND ENCOURAGEMENT

This verse is a joyful invitation to live with a heart anchored in praise. It reminds us that joy is not reserved only for moments when life feels easy; it is cultivated in the act of seeking God. When you seek Him, gladness follows because His presence brings reassurance, strength, and hope. To rejoice in the Lord is to shift focus from circumstance to source. It is a conscious decision to magnify God rather than magnify challenges. Praise does not deny reality; it declares that God is greater than what you face. As you lift God higher, your spirit is strengthened, and your perspective is renewed. This passage also highlights the power of continual praise. Saying "Let God be magnified" is not a one-time declaration, but a lifestyle posture. Praise keeps your heart aligned with truth and guards you against discouragement. It reminds you that God is actively involved in your life as a helper, deliverer, and savior. Joy rises where God is honored. As you choose praise, you create space for peace, gratitude, and divine strength to flourish within you.

JOY IS A FETCHER!

PRAYER AND DAILY DECLARATION

HEAVENLY Father, I thank You that as I seek You, joy fills my heart and gladness rises within me. My joy is not rooted in circumstances, but in Your unchanging character. You are my help, my salvation, and my constant source of strength. When I turn my eyes toward You, perspective shifts and hope is renewed. Teach me to magnify You continually, not only when life feels light, but in every season, every transition, and every challenge. Let praise become my first response rather than worry. When uncertainty attempts to distract me, draw me back into worship. When pressure tries to weigh me down, remind me that joy is my strength. Lord, let my praise silence fear. Let my gratitude guard my heart. Let my worship realign my focus. As I magnify You, let every problem shrink in comparison to Your greatness. Today, I decree and declare that I rejoice and am glad in the Lord. My heart is filled with praise. God is magnified in my life, and joy strengthens my spirit. God is my help and salvation. I will not be ruled by anxiety, I will not be overcome by heaviness. I choose worship over worry, I walk forward with gratitude and confidence, knowing that as I praise You, You sustain me, strengthen me, and surround me with peace. My joy is anchored in You, and my praise is a testimony of trust. In Jesus mighty name, Amen.

SCRIPTURE READING

Revelation 3:8 "I know thy works: behold, I have set before thee an open door, and no man can shut it..."

REFLECTION AND ENCOURAGEMENT

This verse is a deep reassurance for the faithful heart, especially in seasons where your strength feels small. God begins by saying, "I know thy works." That means He has not missed your effort, your endurance, your consistency, or your quiet obedience. Heaven has a record of what people may overlook. Then God announces an outcome only He can control: an open door. This door is not created by connection, status, or human approval; it is established by God Himself. That is why it cannot be shut down by opposition, rejection, delays, or limitations. What God authorizes, no man can cancel. Revelation 3:8 also teaches that God honors persistence. He commends those who have kept His word and not denied His name. This means that faithfulness in weakness still carries weight. God is not waiting for perfection. He is honoring your steady, loyal "yes," even when you feel tired or unseen. If you have been praying for access, opportunity, visibility, or advancement, this passage reminds you that God opens doors strategically. The door before you is divinely appointed. Your season is not random; you are stepping into permission, opportunity, and a path prepared by God.

DIVINE ACCESS

ESTABLISHED!

PRAYER AND DAILY DECLARATION

HEAVENLY Father, I thank You that You see me — not just my public victories, but my quiet obedience, my hidden faithfulness, and my perseverance when no one else notices. Nothing about my commitment to You has been overlooked. Even when my strength feels small, You honor my consistency and remember my devotion. I receive the open doors You have set before me. I trust that what You open is intentional, and what You initiate is purposeful. You do not open doors carelessly; You open them in alignment with destiny and preparation. Strengthen me to remain faithful, steady in obedience, committed to Your Word, and loyal to Your name. Grant me discernment to recognize the doors that come from You and the courage to walk through them with humility. Guard my heart from pride in promotion and from fear in opportunity. Let no intimidation, delay, or distraction hinder my progress. Where You grant access, also grant wisdom. Where You give opportunity, also give grace to steward it well. Today, I decree and declare that God has set before me an open door; no one can shut what God has opened. My faithfulness is met with divine opportunity. I walk boldly into God-ordained access and favor. My steps are guided, protected, and established by the Lord. I am not overlooked, I am remembered. I am not delayed, I am positioned. I am not striving, I am authorized. I move forward with confidence and gratitude, trusting that the doors God opens lead me into purpose, growth, and blessing. In Jesus mighty name, Amen.

SCRIPTURE READING

Hebrews 10:7 "Then said I, Lo, I come (in the volume of the book it is written of me,) to do thy will, O God."

REFLECTION AND ENCOURAGEMENT

This verse reflects the posture of a surrendered life, willing, available, and aligned. Jesus embraced God's will not as a burden, but as a mission. It reminds us that God's will is not meant to crush you; it is meant to fulfill purpose and release fruit that blesses others. Hebrews 10:7 also confirms something deeply reassuring: your life is written with intention. "In the volume of the book, it is written of me" speaks to divine design. You are not an accident. Your gifts, assignments, journey, and even seasons of preparation are part of a larger plan authored by God. Obedience is often where clarity is born. Many times, God reveals the next step when you commit to doing His will, not when you demand full understanding first. This verse encourages you to say, "Lord, yes," even when the full path is not yet visible because obedience invites divine direction. When you align your heart with God's will, you step into purpose, peace, and fulfillment. Your obedience becomes a doorway through which God's power flows, and His glory is revealed in and through your life.

HERE I AM, LORD ALIGNED WITH YOUR WILL!

PRAYER AND DAILY DECLARATION

HEAVENLY Father, I come before You with a willing and yielded heart. I surrender my plans, my preferences, my expectations, and my timing. Where I have tried to control outcomes, I release them into Your hands. Align my desires with Your will and reshape my priorities according to Your purpose. Give me a heart that obeys with joy, not reluctance. Remove resistance from my spirit and replace it with readiness. Teach me to trust deeply that Your will is not restrictive, but good, complete, and purposeful. Even when I do not see the full picture, anchor me in the confidence that You are leading wisely and lovingly. Where I have been hesitant, strengthen me with courage. Where I have been distracted, refocus my attention; where I have been uncertain, grant me clarity. Let my life reflect obedience, humility, and quiet confidence. Use me for Your glory. Let my steps produce fruit that blesses others and reflects Your goodness. Guard me from striving and keep me aligned with heaven's rhythm rather than my own urgency. Today, I decree and declare that I am available to do the will of God. My life aligns with God's purpose, my obedience opens doors of clarity and fulfillment, and my steps are ordered and directed by the Lord. God works through my life for His glory. I am surrendered, yet confident; I am yielded yet established. I am aligned, and therefore at peace. I walk forward resting in Your will, trusting that Your direction leads me into lasting impact and eternal significance. In Jesus mighty name, Amen.

SCRIPTURE READING

Isaiah 11:2–3 "And the spirit of the LORD shall rest upon him, the spirit of wisdom and understanding, the spirit of counsel and might, the spirit of knowledge and of the fear of the LORD; And shall make him of quick understanding in the fear of the LORD: and he shall not judge after the sight of his eyes, neither reprove after the hearing of his ears."

REFLECTION AND ENCOURAGEMENT

These verses reveal the fullness of God's Spirit at work in wisdom, understanding, counsel, might, knowledge, and reverence. This is not merely information; it is spiritual capacity. God does not expect you to navigate life by guesswork or emotion alone. He supplies divine insight through His Spirit. This scripture also highlights discernment: not judging only by what is seen or heard. This means your decisions do not have to be driven by appearances, pressure, or popular opinion. God can guide you beneath the surface, revealing motives, timing, and the wisest path forward. The fear of the Lord is not terror; it is reverence, honoring God's voice above all else. When you walk in reverence, your priorities become clearer and your decisions steadier. You begin to choose what matters to God, not merely what feels urgent. This passage assures you that wisdom is not out of reach. God's Spirit equips you for leadership, parenting, business, relationships, and every assignment you carry. The same Spirit that rested upon Christ empowers you to live with clarity, strength, and holy discernment.

LED BY THE SPIRIT
GUIDED WITH WISDOM!

PRAYER AND DAILY DECLARATION

HEAVENLY Father, I thank You for the gift of Your Holy Spirit not as a distant presence, but as my constant Helper, Teacher, and Guide. I ask You to rest upon my life in fresh measure. Saturate my thoughts, my decisions, and my responses with the influence of Your Spirit. Fill me with wisdom and understanding. Grant me counsel in moments of uncertainty and strength when courage is required. Release knowledge rooted in truth and a holy reverence that guards my heart from pride and presumption. Deliver me from confusion, haste, and emotionally driven decisions. Slow my spirit when needed and steady my judgment with divine clarity. Teach me to discern clearly beyond appearances, beyond noise, beyond pressure. Sharpen my spiritual perception so I recognize what aligns with Your will and what does not. Align my heart so that I desire what You desire and reject what distracts me from purpose. Today, I decree and declare that the Spirit of the Lord rests upon me. I receive wisdom and understanding from God. I walk in counsel, might, and discernment. I am guided beyond appearances and pressured opinions. My decisions reflect reverence and alignment with God. I am not led by impulse; I am led by the Spirit. I am not swayed by fear; I am anchored in wisdom. I am not confused; I am illuminated by truth. I move forward with quiet confidence, knowing that You guide me in truth, establish my steps, and equip me to walk in maturity and clarity. In Jesus mighty name, Amen

SCRIPTURE READING

Jeremiah 20:11 "But the LORD is with me as a mighty terrible one: therefore my persecutors shall stumble, and they shall not prevail; they shall be greatly ashamed; for they shall not prosper; their everlasting confusion shall never be forgotten."

REFLECTION AND ENCOURAGEMENT

This verse is a bold reminder that opposition does not cancel God's protection. Jeremiah faced intense persecution, misunderstanding, and pressure, yet his confidence was anchored in one unshakable truth: the Lord was with him. God's presence is not passive; it is powerful, active, and defensive. God is described here as a mighty warrior. That means you are not standing alone, and you are not exposed. Your battles are not decided by the strength of resistance, but by the strength of your Defender. When God stands with you, opposition loses balance, and plans formed against you lose power. This passage also reassures you that intimidation will not have the final word. Those who rise against God's purpose in your life cannot prevail. God protects not only your life, but your calling, reputation, and future. What was meant to shake you will not succeed. This reflection invites you to remain steady and confident. You do not have to strive, explain yourself endlessly, or fear threats. The Lord Himself is your strength. He preserves your purpose, defends your destiny, and ensures that His plan for your life stands firm.

THE LORD STANDS WITH ME!

PRAYER AND DAILY DECLARATION

HEAVENLY Father, I thank You for being with me as a mighty warrior and faithful defender. Your presence is not passive; it is powerful, active, and intentional. I take comfort in knowing that I am not standing alone in any battle. You surround me with authority, and You rise on my behalf with strength I cannot generate on my own. When opposition rises, I choose to stand in faith and not in fear. When intimidation attempts to shake my confidence, I anchor myself in the assurance that You are greater than any force that stands against me. Fight for me where I cannot fight for myself. Guard my heart from anxiety and steady my mind with clarity. Strengthen me to remain calm, focused, and unwavering under pressure. Let Your presence silence every voice of intimidation. Let Your authority dismantle every hidden scheme. Establish my steps firmly in victory and secure my destiny in Your hands. Today, I decree and declare the Lord is with me as a mighty defender. no opposition formed against me shall prevail. Every plot against my destiny collapses. God's purpose stands firm over my life. I walk boldly, protected and strengthened by God. What rises against me will not overtake me, what is spoken against me will not stand. What God has established cannot be overturned. I move forward with confidence, knowing that You stand with me, defend me, and secure my future. My peace is intact, my purpose is guarded, and my victory is anchored in You. In Jesus mighty name, Amen.

SCRIPTURE READING

Galatians 5:22–23 "But the fruit of the Spirit is love, joy, peace, longsuffering, gentleness, goodness, faith, meekness, temperance: against such there is no law."

REFLECTION AND ENCOURAGEMENT

This passage reminds you that spiritual growth is not measured only by what you accomplish, but it is revealed by what you become. The fruit of the Spirit is the evidence of a life being shaped by God from the inside out. It is not the product of striving harder; it is the result of abiding deeper. Fruit grows gradually. It develops through seasons sometimes quietly, sometimes slowly, but always intentionally. God is not only concerned with your outward progress; He is forming Christlike character within you. Love that remains steady. Joy that is not dependent on circumstances. Peace that guards your heart. Patience that withstands pressure. Gentleness that reflects strength under control. Galatians 5:22–23 also assures you that God's Spirit produces what human willpower cannot consistently maintain. When the Holy Spirit is leading you, He softens what is harsh, strengthens what is weak, and matures what is immature. Where you once reacted in fear, you begin to respond in faith. Where you struggled with self-control, you begin to walk in discipline and wisdom. This is deeply encouraging because it means you are not stuck. Your story is still being shaped. Every day you submit to the Spirit, the fruit becomes more visible. God is growing you into a living reflection of Christ, steady, fruitful, and full of grace.

FRUITFUL AND TRANSFORMED!

PRAYER AND DAILY DECLARATION

HEAVENLY Father, I thank You for the gift of the Holy Spirit living within me not as a distant influence, but as an active, transforming presence. I surrender my attitudes, my reactions, my impulses, and my desires to Your refining work. Where my flesh is quick to respond, slow me. Where my emotions are unstable, steady me. Where I am weak, strengthen me from within. Grow in me what I cannot manufacture on my own. Shape my heart so that Christ is reflected in my thoughts, my words, and my daily conduct. Let love replace fear and defensiveness. Let joy rise even when circumstances are not ideal. Let peace silence anxiety and quiet every internal storm. Cultivate patience when I am tested. Develop gentleness when I am misunderstood. Establish goodness and integrity in my character. Increase faith when I cannot see clearly. Strengthen humility and self-control in every decision. Make my life fruitful and consistent, not emotional and occasional, but rooted and steady. Let my spiritual growth be evident, not in performance, but in transformation. Today, I decree and declare that the fruit of the Spirit is growing in my life. Love, joy, and peace fill my heart and home. Patience and gentleness guide my responses. Goodness and faith mark my character. Humility and self-control strengthen my walk. I am not reacting from impulse; I am responding from the Spirit. I am not driven by emotion, I am formed by grace. I am not stagnant; I am being transformed. I yield fully to the Spirit and trust You to complete the good work You have begun in me, forming Christ within me day by day. In Jesus mighty name, Amen.

SCRIPTURE READING

REFLECTION AND ENCOURAGEMENT

This verse is a prayer of humility and surrender. It acknowledges that God's way is higher than your way, and His paths are wiser than your preferences. David is not merely asking for information, he is asking for formation. "Show me Your ways" speaks to God's character, His principles, and His perspective. "Teach me Your paths" speaks to daily steps and practical direction. Many people seek guidance only when they feel stuck, but this verse invites you to live as a continual student of God. When you allow the Lord to teach you, He trains your discernment. You begin to recognize His leading not only in major decisions, but in everyday moments, conversations, timing, relationships, and opportunities. This scripture passage also reassures you that God is not withholding direction. He delights in leading those who seek Him sincerely. When you ask Him to teach you, He answers through His Word, through peace in your spirit, through wise counsel, and through doors He opens or closes. God's guidance does not confuse; it clarifies. It does not rush; it establishes. If you have been uncertain, overwhelmed, or tired of guessing, let this verse comfort you: you do not have to lead yourself. God guides gently, faithfully, and with perfect understanding of where you are and where you are going.

TEACH ME YOUR WAYS, O LORD!

PRAYER AND DAILY DECLARATION

HEAVENLY Father, I come before You with a humble and teachable heart. I acknowledge that I do not always know the best way, but I trust completely that You do. Your wisdom is higher than my reasoning, and Your perspective is clearer than my own. Shape my thinking according to Your truth and align my desires with what pleases You. Show me Your ways — not only in direction, but in character. Teach me Your paths not only in decisions, but in posture. Direct my steps with clarity and peace so that I move confidently without striving. Remove confusion from my mind and impatience from my heart. Deliver me from leaning on my own understanding when it conflicts with Your truth. Let Your Word be my compass when emotions fluctuate. Let Your peace be my confirmation when choices arise. I desire to be led, not driven. Guided, not pressured. Anchored, not hurried. Today, I decree and declare that the Lord is showing me His ways. God is teaching me His paths. My steps are ordered by the Lord. Confusion is replaced with clarity and peace. I walk forward guided by God's wisdom. I am not rushed, I am directed. I am not uncertain, I am instructed. I am not lost, I am led. I trust You to lead me faithfully, step by step, into purpose, stability, and peace. In Jesus mighty name, Amen.

SCRIPTURE READING

REFLECTION AND ENCOURAGEMENT

These verses reveal a heart that understands the power of gratitude. David praises God freely, not because he is forced, but because he has seen God's goodness firsthand. This is worship that flows from remembrance. It is praise that rises not only in comfort, but also after conflict. This scripture passage teaches that thanksgiving is more than a response; it is a weapon. When you praise God, you shift your focus from the size of the trouble to the strength of your Deliverer. You acknowledge that God is not only present in trouble. He is powerful enough to bring you out of it. Notice the phrase "out of all trouble." This reminds you that God's deliverance is not partial. He does not rescue halfway. He completes what He starts. He brings you through, not just into. When God delivers you, your life becomes visible evidence of His faithfulness. If you have survived what should have broken you, come through what felt heavy, or been protected from danger you never even saw, this passage invites you to respond with praise. Gratitude honors God and strengthens your faith for what lies ahead.

PRAISE BREAKS FORTH!

PRAYER AND DAILY DECLARATION

HEAVENLY Father, I thank You for Your goodness and Your saving power. Thank You for the deliverances I saw clearly and for the ones I never knew were happening. Thank You for carrying me through seasons of pressure, fear, and uncertainty. When I felt surrounded, You were my shield. When I felt weak, You were my strength. When I did not know the way forward, You preserved my steps. Lord, I offer You praise freely — not because every moment was easy, but because You have proven Yourself faithful. You have never abandoned me, never overlooked me, and never failed to sustain me. Teach my heart to remain grateful not only when life feels light, but especially as You bring me through difficulty. Let thanksgiving stay on my lips and worship remain steady in my spirit. Guard me from forgetfulness. Let remembrance fuel my confidence. Let past deliverance strengthen present trust. Today, I decree and declare that the Lord has delivered me out of all trouble. Thanksgiving continually fills my mouth. God is my victory and my defense. My life testifies to God's saving power. Gratitude anchors my heart. What once threatened me did not prevail, what once pressed me did not break me, what once surrounded me did not overtake me. I walk forward strengthened by remembrance, anchored in gratitude, and confident in Your continued faithfulness. The God who delivered me before remains my Defender today and my assurance for tomorrow. In Jesus mighty name, Amen.

SCRIPTURE READING

Psalm 2:7–9 "I will declare the decree: the LORD hath said unto me, Thou art my Son; this day have I begotten thee. Ask of me, and I shall give thee the heathen for thine inheritance, and the uttermost parts of the earth for thy possession. Thou shalt break them with a rod of iron; thou shalt dash them in pieces like a potter's vessel."

REFLECTION AND ENCOURAGEMENT

These verses reveal the power of God's decree. A decree is not a suggestion it is a divine statement backed by authority. God establishes identity ("Thou art my Son"), releases access ("Ask of me"), and assigns inheritance ("I shall give thee…"). This passage shows that God's word confers position, promise, and authority. While Psalm 2 points prophetically to Christ, it also teaches a vital principle for believers: God is the One who defines you, and God is the One who grants what you cannot obtain by human effort alone. You are invited to ask not from desperation, but from a relationship. Asking is not a weakness; it is alignment. It is acknowledging God as Source and Lord. This passage also reminds you that opposition is not equal to God. What resists God's purpose will not endure. When God's decree is active, barriers break, resistance yields, and purpose prevails. You are not governed by fear, intimidation, or limitation; you are governed by God's word. Let this encourage you: you are not powerless, and you are not forgotten. God's promises over your life carry authority. When you pray according to His will, heaven responds with provision, possession, and victory.

ALIGNMENT ROOTED
IN LOVE!

PRAYER AND DAILY DECLARATION

HEAVENLY Father, I thank You for the power of Your Word and the authority of Your decree. What You speak is established. What You declare stands firm. You have defined my identity, assigned my inheritance, and ordered my purpose before I ever understood it. My life is not shaped by opinion or opposition, but by Your eternal counsel. I come before You with faith, not fear, asking according to Your will and trusting fully in Your promises. Teach me to pray boldly without arrogance, to ask confidently without striving, and to receive humbly without pride. Let my petitions align with heaven's intent. Where You have spoken destiny, let it manifest, where You have assigned inheritance, let it be accessed, where You have released promise, let it be established. Break every resistance that stands against Your purpose in my life. Silence every voice that contradicts Your Word. Dismantle every unseen barrier that attempts to delay what You have ordained. Let Your will prevail fully, clearly, and unmistakably. Today, I decree and declare that I stand in the identity God has spoken over me. I ask in faith and receive according to God's will. Divine inheritance and promise are released to me. Opposition breaks under God's authority; God's purpose prevails in my life. I am not defined by delay; I am established by decree. I am not hindered by resistance; I am upheld by authority. I am not uncertain; I am aligned with heaven's will. I stand confident, established, and aligned, knowing that Your decree over my life is final, victorious, and unshakable. In Jesus mighty name, Amen.

SCRIPTURE READING

REFLECTION AND ENCOURAGEMENT

These verses reveal the kind of peace that can only come from God, a peace that remains steady even when opposition surrounds you. David was not writing from a place of comfort. He was facing betrayal, threat, and uncertainty. Yet in the midst of it all, he declared that the Lord was his shield, his glory, and the lifter of his head. A shield represents protection, but God is more than a shield. He is also your glory. This means your worth, dignity, and identity are not diminished by what you are facing. Even when circumstances attempt to press you down, God lifts your head, restores your confidence, and reminds you who you are in Him. One of the most powerful expressions of trust in this passage is David's ability to sleep. Rest in the middle of trouble is evidence of deep faith. It means fear no longer governs your heart or body. God sustains you so fully that even when threats remain, your spirit can remain calm. Psalm 3:3–6 invites you to release the weight of what surrounds you and trust the One who surrounds you. No matter how many voices rise against you, God's presence is greater. You are not exposed. You are not overwhelmed. You are sustained.

THE LORD UPHOLDS ME!

PRAYER AND DAILY DECLARATION

HEAVENLY Father, I thank You for being my shield, my glory, and the lifter of my head. When pressure rises, and fear attempts to overwhelm me, You stand between me and every threat, visible and invisible. You do not merely observe my struggle; You actively guard me, surround me, and sustain me. You restore my confidence when discouragement tries to bow my head. You remind me that I am not defeated, not forgotten, and not exposed. My dignity is preserved in You. My future is secured in You. I surrender every anxious thought, every heavy burden, and every voice of intimidation into Your hands. Silence the noise of fear and steady my heart with Your truth. Teach me to rest fully in You, not only when circumstances shift, but even when they remain unchanged. Let my trust be deeper than my emotions and stronger than my surroundings. Today, I decree and declare that the Lord is my shield on every side. God lifts my head and restores my confidence. Fear has no authority over my peace. I sleep in peace, sustained by the Lord. I am confident, protected, and secure in God. I will not bow to pressure. I will not surrender to anxiety; I will not lose heart in uncertainty. You sustain me by day and guard me by night. My rest is protected, my mind is steadied, and Your faithful presence upholds my heart. I walk forward calm, confident, and covered, knowing that You defend me, sustain me, and lift me continually. In Jesus mighty name, Amen.

SCRIPTURE READING

Isaiah 45:2–3 "I will go before thee, and make the crooked places straight: I will break in pieces the gates of brass, and cut in sunder the bars of iron: And I will give thee the treasures of darkness, and hidden riches of secret places, that thou mayest know that I, the LORD, which call thee by thy name, am the God of Israel."

REFLECTION AND ENCOURAGEMENT

These verses are a powerful assurance that God never sends you forward unprepared. He declares that He goes before you, removing obstacles, correcting misalignment, and dismantling barriers that human effort cannot overcome. Your progress is not dependent on force or struggle, but on God's divine leading. Gates of bronze and bars of iron symbolize resistance, limitation, and closed systems. God does not negotiate with obstacles. He breaks them. What has felt immovable, intimidating, or delayed for years can be dismantled by God in a moment. His power is decisive and complete. Isaiah 45:2–3 also speaks of hidden treasures. These are blessings you did not anticipate: resources, wisdom, access, favor, and provision revealed at the right time. God calls you by name in this promise, reminding you that His guidance is personal. You are not forgotten, overlooked, or wandering without direction. This passage reassures you that your journey is ordered. You are not guessing your way forward. God is already working ahead of you, opening doors, releasing provision, and making it unmistakably clear that He is the One leading you.

HIDDEN TREASURES
REVEALED!

PRAYER AND DAILY DECLARATION

HEAVENLY Father, I thank You that You go before me and prepare the way. You are never reacting to my future. You are already there, arranging what I cannot see and aligning what I cannot control. You remove obstacles I cannot move and open doors I could never unlock on my own. Even when the path is not fully visible, I trust Your leading. When I do not understand the timing, I trust Your wisdom. Break every barrier that resists Your purpose in my life. Dismantle delays that are not ordained by You. Straighten what has been crooked. Clarify what has been confusing. Reveal what has been hidden and bring light to every unseen opportunity. Let provision meet me at the point of obedience. Let favor accompany my steps. Let opportunities unfold in divine timing. Where there were limitations, release expansion. Where there are closed paths, create new access. Today, I decree and declare that God goes before me. Every crooked place is made straight; barriers are broken by God's power. Hidden treasures are revealed to me, and divine provision meets my obedience. I am not wandering; I am being led. I am not delayed; I am being positioned. I am not uncertain; I am being prepared. I walk confidently, called and guided by God. I move forward assured, strengthened, and expectant, knowing that You have already prepared what lies ahead and established the path beneath my feet. In Jesus mighty name, Amen

SCRIPTURE READING

Proverbs 3:24 "When thou liest down, thou shalt not be afraid: yea, thou shalt lie down, and thy sleep shall be sweet."

REFLECTION AND ENCOURAGEMENT

This verse reveals God's heart for your rest. Rest is not a reward for finishing everything; it is a gift rooted in trust. God does not intend for your nights to be filled with anxiety, replaying worries, or restless thoughts. He promises peace that guards you even while you sleep. Fear often speaks loudest in quiet moments. When distractions fade, concerns try to rise. Yet Proverbs 3:24 reassures you that when your confidence is anchored in the Lord, fear loses its grip. You can lie down without dread because God remains awake, watching over you. Sweet sleep is more than physical rest; it is emotional and spiritual peace. It is the ability to release control and trust God with what cannot be solved overnight. When you surrender the day into God's hands, you rest in the assurance that He is faithful to handle what you cannot. Let this truth settle your heart: God is not asking you to carry tomorrow's burdens through the night. You are safe. You are covered. You are permitted to rest deeply in His care.

REST IS A GIFT FROM GOD!

PRAYER AND DAILY DECLARATION

HEAVENLY Father, I thank You for the gift of peace and sacred rest. You designed my body and soul to be renewed in Your presence, and I choose to enter that rest with trust. I release every anxious thought, unresolved concern, unfinished task, and heavy emotion into Your hands. What I cannot resolve tonight, I entrust to You. You are faithful to guard me even while I sleep. While my eyes close, Yours remain open. Quiet my racing thoughts. Slow my breathing. Calm my heart. Let Your presence settle over my home like a covering. Teach me to trust You fully, not only in active moments of faith during the day, but in surrendered rest through the night. Remove every trace of fear from my atmosphere. Silence internal noise. Let Your peace regulate my mind and bring ease to my body. I receive the rest You promise, not shallow rest, but deep, restorative peace. Today, I decree and declare that fear has no place in my rest. My sleep is peaceful and sweet. God watches over me continually. My heart rests in divine security. Peace fills my mind and body. I am covered. I am not restless, I am settled. I am not unguarded, I am protected. I lay down in confidence and rise refreshed, strengthened, and upheld by Your unfailing care. Night does not weaken me; it restores me under Your watchful love. In Jesus mighty name, Amen.

SCRIPTURE READING

Genesis 1:29 "And God said, Behold, I have given you every herb bearing seed… to you it shall be for meat."

REFLECTION AND ENCOURAGEMENT

This verse reveals God as a generous Provider from the very beginning. Before humanity ever encountered need or lack, God had already prepared provision. His giving was intentional, sufficient, and sustaining. God did not create you and then leave you to figure life out on your own. He planned for your needs in advance. Genesis 1:29 also shows that God's provision carries purpose. Every seed-bearing plant speaks of sustainability, continuity, and future increase. God provides in ways that meet present needs while also holding potential for tomorrow. What He gives today is designed to multiply, endure, and sustain over time. This passage invites you to trust God not only as your Provider, but also as your Sustainer. Your life is not dependent on chance, economy, or uncertainty; it is held within God's intentional care. Even when seasons change, His faithfulness remains constant. As you receive what God gives, you are also invited into stewardship. Gratitude, obedience, and trust allow you to experience provision with peace rather than anxiety. God's supply is not meant to create fear; it is meant to cultivate confidence in His goodness.

PROVISION PRECEDED
THE NEED!

PRAYER AND DAILY DECLARATION

HEAVENLY Father, I thank You for Your generous and faithful provision. Before I ever recognized the need, You had already prepared the supply. Nothing in my life catches You off guard. You are not reacting to my circumstances, You are sustaining me through them with wisdom and intention. I trust You as my Provider and Sustainer in every season, in times of abundance, and in moments that stretch my faith. Teach me to steward what You place in my hands with wisdom, discipline, and gratitude. Guard my heart from waste, comparison, and striving. Let me manage increase with humility and handle responsibility with integrity. Remove every fear of lack from my heart. Silence the anxiety that whispers scarcity. Replace it with quiet confidence in Your covenant care. Where worry once lingered, let trust take root. Where uncertainty once rose, let assurance stand firm. Today, I decree and declare that God has already provided for my needs. My life is sustained by God's goodness. I steward God's provision wisely. Fear of lack has no place in my heart; I live under God's faithful care. I am not abandoned to uncertainty, I am not subject to scarcity, I am upheld by divine supply. I walk forward secure, grateful, and confident, knowing that You have prepared provision ahead of me and that Your faithfulness will sustain me fully. In Jesus mighty name, Amen.

SCRIPTURE READING

Luke 10:19 "Behold, I give unto you power to tread on serpents and scorpions, and over all the power of the enemy: and nothing shall by any means hurt you."

REFLECTION AND ENCOURAGEMENT

This verse is a clear reminder that you do not walk through life defenseless. Jesus speaks with authority and gives authority. This power is not something you earn through effort or maturity; it is a gift released through a relationship with Him. Luke 10:19 declares that every form of spiritual opposition is already subject to Christ's authority. While challenges may arise, they do not govern your destiny. God has placed authority in your hands to walk with confidence, discernment, and spiritual security. This authority is not rooted in self-confidence, but in God's promise. You are protected because God has spoken it. His covering establishes boundaries that opposition cannot cross. What God has secured, no enemy can override. Let this truth strengthen your faith: you are not vulnerable, powerless, or exposed. You are empowered through Christ, guarded by God, and sustained by divine protection. You walk forward under heaven's authority.

AUTHORITY THROUGH CHRIST!

PRAYER AND DAILY DECLARATION

HEAVENLY Father, I thank You for the authority You have given me through Christ. This authority is not rooted in my strength, but in His victory. I stand confident in Your protection and in the power of Your unchanging Word. Because of Christ, I am not standing from a place of defense, but from a place of triumph. I reject fear, intimidation, and every subtle suggestion that I am vulnerable or unguarded. I walk in spiritual authority, not striving for power, but resting in what has already been secured. Your covering surrounds me. Your promises defend me. Your Spirit strengthens me from within. Where opposition attempts to rise, it finds its limit in You. Where intimidation attempts to speak, it is silenced by truth. Nothing is permitted to harm or derail me outside of Your sovereign allowance. I am preserved under covenant care. Today, I decree and declare that I walk in God-given authority. Every form of opposition is under Christ. I am divinely protected on every side. Fear has no power over my life. Victory defines my position. I am not intimidated; I am established. I am not threatened, I am covered. I am not uncertain; I am secured in Christ. I move forward secure, bold, and assured, knowing that Your power surrounds me, Your Spirit sustains me, and Your authority upholds my life. In Jesus mighty name, Amen.

SCRIPTURE READING

REFLECTION AND ENCOURAGEMENT

This verse reveals God as the careful and intentional Gardener of your life. He watches over what grows within you and around you. Anything that does not originate from Him, misaligned beliefs, unhealthy patterns, limiting mindsets, or harmful influences does not have permission to remain. Uprooting can feel uncomfortable because it involves change, release, and sometimes loss. But divine uprooting is never punishment; it is protection. God removes what competes with truth so that what He has planted can grow unhindered. What He uproots is not meant to harm you; it is meant to preserve your future. Matthew 15:13 reminds you that alignment often requires removal before expansion. God is committed to what lasts. What He plants is rooted in truth, sustained by grace, and designed to bear fruit in every season. This passage invites you to trust the pruning process. You are not being stripped, you are being strengthened. As God uproots what is not from Him, He creates space for clarity, peace, and lasting growth.

ROOTED TO FLOURISH!

PRAYER AND DAILY DECLARATION

HEAVENLY Father, I thank You for caring deeply about what grows in my life. You are not passive about my development; You are attentive, intentional, and faithful as the Gardener of my heart. Nothing in me escapes Your notice. You see what is fruitful and what is harmful. You know what must remain and what must be removed. I surrender fully to Your work of alignment. Search my heart and reveal anything that competes with Your truth. Uproot every thought, habit, attachment, mindset, or influence that was not planted by You. Remove hidden roots of fear, pride, insecurity, bitterness, or distraction. Prune what is excessive. Strengthen what is weak. Nourish what is aligned with Your purpose. Even when Your refining feels stretching, let Your peace steady me. Help me trust that every pruning makes room for greater fruit. Where You remove, You also restore. Where You cut away, You also cultivate. Today, I decree and declare that everything not planted by God is uprooted. My life is aligned with God's truth. What God has planted in me will flourish. My heart is free, healed, and fruitful. God's purpose in me will remain and grow. I am not overgrown, I am cultivated. I am not barren; I am being prepared. I am not shaken; I am deeply rooted. I stand rooted, aligned, and confident, knowing that what You plant will endure, mature, and bear lasting fruit in every season. In Jesus mighty name, Amen.

SCRIPTURE READING

REFLECTION AND ENCOURAGEMENT

This passage boldly declares that no captivity is beyond God's power. It confronts what appears irreversible and answers it with divine authority; deliverance is certain. What seems permanently lost, stolen, or held by force is not out of God's reach. This scripture passage reveals that God does not merely sympathize with your struggle; He intervenes. He does not watch passively while injustice continues. He steps in as a Warrior and a Redeemer. When God says, "I will contend," it means the battle shifts from your hands to His. This passage is deeply personal. God does not generalize the promise; He makes it specific. "I will contend with him that contendeth with thee." God addresses what is opposing you. He confronts resistance directly and rescues what was taken, including what concerns your future and your legacy. This reflection invites you to release hopelessness and fatigue. You are not fighting alone. You are not abandoned in the struggle. God Himself is engaged on your behalf, and His involvement guarantees redemption, restoration, and victory.

THE LORD WILL CONTEND FOR ME!

PRAYER AND DAILY DECLARATION

HEAVENLY Father, I thank You that You fight for me. You are my Deliverer, my Redeemer, and the One who restores what was broken or taken. Nothing in my life is beyond Your reach. No delay is too long, no loss too great, no captivity too strong for Your power to overturn. I place every captive area of my life into Your hands — every place of loss, restriction, disappointment, or prolonged struggle. Where progress felt blocked, where joy felt diminished, where opportunity seemed withheld, I invite Your intervention. Contend on my behalf. Confront what confronts me. Break every chain that has attempted to limit what You ordained. Lord, redeem time that feels wasted. Restore the strength that was drained. Reclaim ground that seemed lost. Let Your justice speak where there was injustice. Let Your freedom replace every form of bondage. Today, I decree and declare that every area of my life once held captive is delivered. God contends with those who contend with me. Restoration is released into my life. No force is greater than God's power; redemption is active in my story. What was restrained is being released, what was delayed is being restored, and what was contested is being secured. I walk in freedom, redemption, and victory. I stand confident and at peace, knowing that the Lord Himself fights for me, establishes my boundaries, and secures my future. In Jesus mighty name, Amen.

SCRIPTURE READING

Hosea 6:3 "Then shall we know, if we follow on to know the LORD: his going forth is prepared as the morning; and he shall come unto us as the rain, as the latter and former rain unto the earth."

REFLECTION AND ENCOURAGEMENT

This verse is an invitation into intentional pursuit. Knowing the Lord is not a single encounter; it is a continual journey. Hosea reminds us that spiritual growth happens when we keep going, even when understanding feels incomplete or progress feels slow. Persistence in seeking God deepens the relationship and clarity over time. God's faithfulness is compared to the morning. Just as dawn arrives without fail, God's presence is dependable. He is not inconsistent or unpredictable. When you pursue Him, you are not chasing uncertainty; you are meeting steadfast faithfulness that is already prepared to meet you. The imagery of rain speaks of refreshment and renewal. God does not come empty-handed. He comes nourishing dry places, restoring strength, and reviving what has grown weary. Former and latter rain point to the complete provision of what you needed before and what you need now. Even seasons of dryness are not permanent when God releases His presence. This passage reassures you that pursuit is never wasted. When you seek God faithfully, He responds faithfully. Growth may be quiet and gradual, but it is always purposeful. God meets consistency with renewal and pursuit with presence.

RAIN UPON DRY GROUND!

PRAYER AND DAILY DECLARATION

HEAVENLY Father, I choose to pursue You with intention and steady faith. Not casually, not occasionally, but with a heart that longs to know You more. Teach me to remain consistent in seeking You, even when answers feel delayed and progress feels quiet. When I do not see immediate results, anchor me in the truth that You are still working. I trust Your faithfulness and Your timing. You are never late, never distracted, never indifferent to my pursuit. Refresh my spirit like rain upon dry ground. Where I have felt weary, pour out renewal. Where I have felt stagnant, stir fresh life. Deepen my understanding so that I do not merely know about You but walk closely with You. Let my relationship with You grow steady, rooted, and alive, not driven by emotion alone but sustained by devotion and trust. Guard me from spiritual fatigue and keep my heart soft toward Your voice. Today, I decree and declare that I pursue the Lord faithfully. God meets me with renewal and refreshment. My spirit is revived by God's presence. Growth and understanding increase in my life. God's faithfulness sustains me daily. I am not dry, I am being watered, I am not stagnant, I am growing, I am not unseen, I am met by God. I continue forward with confidence, knowing that as I pursue You, You meet me with life, clarity, strength, and renewal. In Jesus mighty name, Amen.

SCRIPTURE READING

Deuteronomy 11:14 "That I will give you the rain of your land in his due season, the first rain and the latter rain, that thou mayest gather in thy corn, and thy wine, and thine oil."

REFLECTION AND ENCOURAGEMENT

This verse highlights God's intentional timing. He sends rain not randomly, not late, and not early, but in due season. God understands the rhythm of growth and the process required for harvest. He knows when the ground is ready and when the seed needs watering. Obedience positions you for provision. God's blessings flow in alignment with His will, not hurried by pressure or delayed by doubt. Every season you walk through has purpose. What feels slow is often preparation. What feels quiet is often cultivation. Deuteronomy 11:14 reassures you that waiting is not neglect. God is attentive to your land, your work, your prayers, your obedience, and your faithfulness. He sees the seed you have planted and the labor you have invested. When the time is right, He releases exactly what is needed for growth and increase. Trusting God's timing brings peace. You do not have to force outcomes or compare seasons. God knows when to send rain, and when He does, it produces abundance that is complete and lasting.

RAIN IN DUE SEASON!

PRAYER AND DAILY DECLARATION

HEAVENLY Father, I trust Your timing and Your provision. You are not hurried, and You are not delayed. Every season in my life is under Your careful supervision. Teach me to remain faithful and obedient while I wait. Guard my heart from frustration, comparison, and premature striving. Help me to understand that waiting with You is never wasted. Let me rest in the assurance that You are attentive to every detail — every prayer, every act of obedience, every quiet sacrifice. You see the seed sown in faith, even when the ground appears still. You are the Lord of seasons, and You send rain at the appointed time. I receive the rain You send in its proper season. I trust You to bring growth where there was barrenness, increase where there was lack, and fruitfulness where there was once delay. Strengthen my patience and keep my expectations alive. Let my waiting be marked by trust, not tension. Today, I decree and declare that God releases provision in due season. My obedience positions me for blessing; my land is fruitful and productive. God's timing is perfect for my life; harvest follows every faithful season of waiting. I am not forgotten; I am being cultivated. I am not delayed; I am being prepared. I am not barren; I am positioned for increase. I remain steady, trusting that You will send rain at the appointed time and crown my season with growth, abundance, and fulfillment. In Jesus mighty name, Amen.

SCRIPTURE READING

REFLECTION AND ENCOURAGEMENT

This verse reveals the far-reaching nature of God's mercy not only toward the one who was sick, but toward everyone connected to him. Paul acknowledges that God's intervention spared Epaphroditus from death, yet he also recognizes that this same mercy shielded his own heart from unbearable grief. God's mercy is never isolated; it flows through relationships, families, and spiritual connections. Mercy is God's compassionate response to human fragility. It steps in where strength fails, where doctors' reports grow heavy, and where situations appear irreversible. Philippians 2:27 reminds us that sickness, loss, and near-death moments do not have the final word. God does. His mercy interrupts tragedy and rewrites outcomes. This verse also reveals God's sensitivity to emotional weight. "Sorrow upon sorrow" speaks of compounded grief pain layered upon pain, loss stacked upon exhaustion. God does not dismiss this reality. His mercy moves ahead of devastation, preventing the overflow of sorrow that could overwhelm the soul. He heals bodies, yes but He also preserves hearts. Let this truth comfort you: God sees what you are carrying. He knows the silent fears, the anxious prayers, and the dread of loss you may not speak aloud. His mercy is timely, intentional, and deeply personal. Where sorrow could have multiplied, mercy intervenes. Where despair threatened to settle, restoration begins.

MERCY PRESERVES US!

PRAYER AND DAILY DECLARATION

HEAVENLY Father, I thank You for Your mercy that preserves life and restores hope. Your compassion is not distant or passive; it is active, attentive, and powerful. You see moments of weakness, sickness, and vulnerability, and You respond with kindness and intervention. Where sorrow could have multiplied, You stepped in. Where fear tried to settle, You released peace. Thank You for protecting not only bodies, but hearts. Thank You for guarding minds, sustaining emotions, and strengthening weary spirits. Your mercy reaches unseen places and holds what feels fragile. Lord, I trust Your mercy to sustain me and everyone connected to me, my family, my loved ones, and those I carry in prayer. Cover our homes with compassion. Surround our health with protection. Guard our hearts from despair. Let Your mercy speak louder than every threat. Today, I decree and declare that God's mercy preserves my life. Sorrow will not overwhelm my heart. God intervenes on my behalf. Mercy surrounds me and my loved ones. Life, healing, and restoration prevail. We are not abandoned, we are covered, we are not vulnerable, we are preserved, we are not overcome, we are upheld by mercy. I rest in Your compassion, confident that You are near, attentive, and faithful. Your mercy sustains today and secures tomorrow. In Jesus mighty name, Amen.

SCRIPTURE READING

REFLECTION AND ENCOURAGEMENT

This verse reveals the purpose of God's anointing. Jesus declares that the Spirit of the Lord rests upon Him not for display, recognition, or status but for assignment. God's anointing is always functional. It is released to bring transformation where there is brokenness and hope where there has been despair. Luke 4:18 shows that the Spirit of God is active and intentional. The anointing carries good news to the brokenhearted, liberty to the captive, sight to the blind, and release to the oppressed. This was not limited to Jesus' earthly ministry; it reveals the ongoing work of God's Spirit through His people. Wherever the Spirit rests, restoration follows. This verse reminds you that you are not anointed without purpose. God does not place His Spirit casually. Where He anoints, He empowers. Where He sends, He equips. Your life is marked with divine intention, and your obedience activates the assignment attached to the anointing. Be encouraged: the same Spirit that empowered Christ now works within you. You carry the presence of God into spaces of pain, confusion, and bondage. Through your words, prayers, actions, and compassion, God releases freedom, healing, and light wherever He sends you.

ANOINTED, APPOINTED, FREE!

PRAYER AND DAILY DECLARATION

HEAVENLY Father, I thank You for the anointing of Your Spirit upon my life. Your presence is not accidental or symbolic. It is empowering, intentional, and purposeful. You have marked me with grace for an assignment that reflects Your heart. Thank You for clothing me with compassion, wisdom, and spiritual authority through Your Spirit. Let Your Spirit work through me to bring healing where there is brokenness, freedom where there is bondage, and hope where there is despair. Guard me from self-reliance and keep me dependent on Your leading. Where I feel inadequate, remind me that the anointing is sufficient. Where I feel uncertain, steady me with clarity. Align me daily with the assignment You have entrusted to me. Refine my motives, strengthen my obedience, and enlarge my capacity to serve faithfully. Let my life be a vessel of restoration, truth, and love, not for recognition, but for Your glory. Today, I decree and declare that the Spirit of the Lord is upon me. I am anointed for a divine purpose. Healing and freedom flow through my life. God uses me to restore and uplift others. I walk confidently in my God-given assignment. I am not operating in my own strength; I am empowered by the Spirit. I am not walking alone; I am commissioned by heaven. I am not without purpose; I am sent with intention. I yield fully to Your Spirit and embrace the sacred work You have entrusted to me. Let my life reflect Your power, Your compassion, and Your truth wherever I am sent. In Jesus mighty name, Amen.

SCRIPTURE READING

REFLECTION AND ENCOURAGEMENT

This verse is a heartfelt prayer for divine favor and permanence. Moses recognizes that human effort alone is fragile, temporary, and incomplete without God's involvement. He asks not only for success, but for God's beauty. His grace, presence, and approval rest upon His people. Psalm 90:17 teaches us that true productivity flows from God's favor. When God establishes the work of our hands, He gives it weight, endurance, and meaning. What He establishes lasts beyond effort, beyond seasons, and beyond human strength. This is the difference between labor that exhausts and work that endures. The repetition in this verse emphasizes dependence. "Establish the work of our hands" is both a request and a surrender, an acknowledgment that without God, even our best efforts can fade. With Him, however, ordinary work becomes significant and temporary efforts become legacy. Let this verse encourage you: your labor is seen by God. When His beauty rests upon you, your work is covered in grace, marked by excellence, and sustained by His power. God delights in giving permanence to what is committed to Him.

THE LORD ESTABLISHES MY WORK!

PRAYER AND DAILY DECLARATION

HEAVENLY Father, I thank You for Your beauty, grace, and favor upon my life. Your presence is what gives meaning to my effort and weight to my work. Without You, my labor is temporary and incomplete. But with You, it becomes established, sustained, and significant. Let Your presence rest upon me and upon all that I put my hands to. Breathe upon my ideas, my responsibilities, my leadership, and my daily tasks. Refine my motives, align my intentions, and ensure that what I build reflects Your character and truth. Establish my labor according to Your will. Strengthen what is aligned with You. Remove what is not. Make my work fruitful, meaningful, and enduring beyond temporary results. Let what I produce carry integrity, excellence, and impact. May my assignments reflect both diligence and dependence on You. Today, I decree and declare that the beauty of the Lord rests upon my life. God establishes the work of my hands. My efforts are sustained by divine favor, and my work produces a lasting impact. What God establishes in my life shall endure. I do not labor in vain; I am not building alone, I am not striving without support. I labor with peace, confidence, and trust in Your sustaining power. What You bless will flourish, what You establish will stand, what You breathe upon will endure. In Jesus mighty name, Amen.

SCRIPTURE READING

Isaiah 53:5 "But he was wounded for our transgressions, he was bruised for our iniquities: the chastisement of our peace was upon him; and with his stripes we are healed."

REFLECTION AND ENCOURAGEMENT

This verse reveals the depth of Christ's sacrifice and the completeness of what was purchased for us. Isaiah speaks prophetically of Jesus, showing that His suffering was not accidental. It was intentional and redemptive. Every wound carried purpose. Every stripe released healing. Isaiah 53:5 reminds us that Jesus addressed the whole person. He was wounded for sin, bruised for brokenness, chastised so we could have peace, and stripped so we could be healed. Nothing about your pain, spiritual, emotional, or physical, was overlooked at the cross. Peace here is more than calm feelings; it is wholeness, restoration, and right alignment with God. Healing is not only a future hope. It is a present provision. What Jesus bore was enough to cover guilt, restore identity, and mend what life has fractured. Let this verse anchor your faith: your healing was paid for, your peace was secured, and your restoration was intentional. You are not waiting for God to notice your pain. He already responded through Christ.

REDEEMED AND MADE WHOLE!

PRAYER AND DAILY DECLARATION

HEAVENLY Father, I thank You for the finished work of Jesus Christ. Nothing was left incomplete at the cross. Through His sacrifice, forgiveness was secured, peace was established, and healing was made available. What He accomplished was full, final, and sufficient. Thank You that through His suffering, I receive reconciliation with You. Thank You that shame was carried, condemnation was silenced, and separation was removed. I do not strive to earn what has already been purchased. I receive by faith what Christ has already secured. Today, I release every burden, every lingering pain, every emotional wound, and every physical affliction into Your hands. Let the power of the cross speak into every broken place. Let Your healing flow through my body, renew my mind, and restore my spirit. Where there was fragmentation, bring wholeness. Where there was unrest, establish peace. Today, I decree and declare that Jesus bore my pain and my sin. Peace has been restored to my life, by His stripes I am healed. Wholeness flows through every area of my life, and I walk in the fullness of Christ's finished work. I am not condemned, I am forgiven. I am not broken, I am restored. I am not distant; I am reconciled through Christ. I rest in Your love and trust fully in the power of the cross. What Jesus completed, I receive. What He redeemed, I walk in. What He restored, I embrace. In Jesus mighty name, Amen.

SCRIPTURE READING

REFLECTION AND ENCOURAGEMENT

This verse affirms the absolute reliability of God's Word. Isaiah declares that nothing God has spoken will fail, not one promise, not one instruction, not one purpose. Heaven and earth may change, but what God has commanded stands firm and complete. Isaiah 34:16 reminds us that God's Word is intentional and precise. "None shall want her mate" speaks of completeness; nothing God ordains is lacking, unfinished, or abandoned. What He speaks is sustained by His Spirit until it comes together exactly as He intended. This passage also invites active engagement: seek and read. God calls His people to search His Word because truth brings clarity, confidence, and assurance. When circumstances feel uncertain or delayed, Scripture anchors the heart in what cannot fail. Be encouraged, God's promises are not fragile. They do not depend on circumstance, timing, or human ability. What His mouth has commanded, His Spirit actively gathers, aligns, and fulfills. If God has spoken concerning your life, it will come together.

GOD'S WORD

NEVER FAILS!

PRAYER AND DAILY DECLARATION

HEAVENLY Father, I thank You for the truth and unshakable certainty of Your Word. What You have spoken carries authority. What You have declared cannot be reversed. Your promises are not fragile, and Your purposes are not temporary. Heaven and earth may shift, but Your Word remains established. Help me to seek You diligently through Scripture, not casually, but with hunger and reverence. Let Your Word shape my thinking, steady my emotions, and anchor my expectations. Strengthen my faith to trust what You have said, even when fulfillment is still unfolding, and circumstances have not yet aligned. Teach me to stand firm in the space between promise and manifestation. Remind me that delay does not cancel decree. Your Spirit is actively working, aligning, preparing, and positioning all things according to Your perfect will. Today, I decree and declare that God's Word over my life will not fail. Every promise spoken by God is fulfilled. Nothing God has ordained for me is missing. God's Spirit aligns all things for my good. I trust fully in the certainty of God's Word. I am not standing on opinion; I am standing on promise. I am not shaken by delay; I am anchored in decree. I am not uncertain; I am established in truth. I stand firm and confident, knowing that what God has spoken shall surely come to pass, and what He has begun, He will faithfully complete. In Jesus mighty name, Amen.

SCRIPTURE READING

Luke 13:11–13 "And, behold, there was a woman which had a spirit of infirmity eighteen years, and was bowed together, and could in no wise lift up herself. And when Jesus saw her, he called her to him, and said unto her, Woman, thou art loosed from thine infirmity. And he laid his hands on her: and immediately she was made straight, and glorified God."

REFLECTION AND ENCOURAGEMENT

This passage reveals the compassionate heart of Jesus toward long-standing pain. The woman had carried her infirmity for eighteen years so long that her condition could have been mistaken for permanence. Yet Jesus did not see her as defined by her condition; He saw her as someone worthy of freedom and restoration. Notice that Jesus saw her. He did not overlook her posture or ignore her pain. He initiated the encounter, called her forward, and spoke release before He touched her. This shows us that restoration often begins with a word from God, truth spoken into places that have been bent by time, burden, or limitation. Jesus declared, "Thou art loosed." Not "you will be loosed someday," but now. This reminds us that what has lingered for years is not too deeply rooted for God to heal. Time does not weaken God's power. Duration does not limit His authority. When Jesus laid His hands on her, the transformation was immediate. What had kept her bowed was broken, and her response was worship. Restoration led to praise. Healing produced testimony. This passage reassures you that God's compassion reaches long-standing struggles, and His touch brings freedom that lifts your head and straightens your path.

HEALED AND RESTORED!

PRAYER AND DAILY DECLARATION

HEAVENLY Father, I thank You for seeing me fully and compassionately. Nothing about my life is hidden from You. You are aware of every silent burden, every prolonged struggle, and every place where I have felt bent under time, pressure, disappointment, or pain. You do not overlook what has weighed on me You respond with mercy and power. Today, I receive Your word of freedom. Speak release over every lingering limitation. Touch every area that has felt restricted, strained, or diminished. Lay Your healing hand upon my life and restore what has been weakened by long seasons of endurance. Where I have adjusted to survival, restore me to strength. Where I have grown accustomed to limitations, I awaken to freedom. I trust not only in gradual change, but in Your power to bring immediate and complete restoration. What has been bound can be loosed. What has been bent can be straightened. What has been burdened can be lifted. Today, I decree and declare that Jesus sees me and calls me forward. I am loosed from every infirmity and burden. Long-standing struggles do not define my future. Restoration lifts my head and straightens my path. My life responds with gratitude and praise. I refuse to carry what Christ has already lifted. I refuse to remain bent where God has spoken freedom. I stand renewed, restored, and strengthened. My posture is upright. My spirit is free. My future is no longer shaped by past affliction but by divine restoration. I glorify You for what You have done and for what You are completing in me. In Jesus mighty name, Amen.

SCRIPTURE READING

REFLECTION AND ENCOURAGEMENT

This verse reveals the extraordinary power of God's Word. Healing and deliverance did not come through effort, struggle, or human intervention; it went through a word sent by God. His Word carries authority, intention, and power to reach places no hand can touch. God sent His Word. That means healing was intentional, not accidental. Deliverance was purposeful, not delayed. Whatever destruction threatened their lives, physical, emotional, or spiritual. God's Word intervened and reversed it. His Word does not merely comfort; it restores and rescues. Psalm 107:20 reminds us that God's Word still works today. It heals hearts wounded by loss, minds burdened by fear, bodies weakened by illness, and lives affected by brokenness. What feels overwhelming to you is not beyond the reach of His Word. This passage encourages you to receive God's Word personally. When He speaks, restoration follows. When His truth enters a situation, destruction loses its hold. God's Word is alive, active, and effective, and it is sent with you in mind.

HEALED AND DELIVERED
BY HIS WORD!

PRAYER AND DAILY DECLARATION

HEAVENLY Father, I thank You for the living power of Your Word. You do not speak casually or without purpose. When You speak, healing is released, restoration begins, and deliverance is set in motion. Your Word carries authority, intention, and divine life. It does not return empty, and it does not fall to the ground without accomplishing what You have sent it to do. Today, I receive every word You have spoken over my life, every promise, every declaration, every instruction. Send Your Word into every area where healing is needed. Let it penetrate places of weakness, discouragement, confusion, and delay. Where destruction has attempted to take root, let Your Word uproot it. Where despair has tried to settle, let Your truth override it. Let Your Word rebuild what has been broken, strengthen what has been weakened, and revive what has felt dormant. I trust that the same Word that created light, calmed storms, and raised the dead is active in my life now. Today, I decree and declare that God's Word brings healing to my life. I am delivered from every form of destruction. God's Word is active, powerful, and effective in me. Restoration follows the Word of the Lord. My life reflects the healing power of God. I stand on what God has spoken. I align my heart with His truth. I expect manifestation according to His decree. I stand healed, delivered, strengthened, and restored by the Word the Lord has sent. What He has spoken over me is unfolding with power and precision. In Jesus mighty name, Amen.

SCRIPTURE READING

Deuteronomy 7:15 "And the LORD will take away from thee all sickness, and will put none of the evil diseases of Egypt, which thou knowest, upon thee; but will lay them upon all them that hate thee."

REFLECTION AND ENCOURAGEMENT

This verse is a strong declaration of God's commitment to the health and preservation of His people. God does not merely reduce sickness. He takes it away. That language speaks of removal, separation, and distance. Sickness is not meant to linger where God has established His covenant of protection. God specifically references the diseases of Egypt to remind His people of what they were delivered from. Egypt represents bondage, affliction, and oppression. By saying these diseases will not come upon you, God is declaring that your past captivity does not get to define your future condition. What once afflicted you no longer has permission to follow you. This promise also highlights distinction. God places a protective boundary around His people. You are not subject to the same outcomes as those outside His covenant. Divine health is not luck. It is in alignment with God's covering and care. Deuteronomy 7:15 reassures you that God is intentional about your well-being. He sees health as part of your inheritance. You are not meant to live under the fear of illness or recurring affliction. God's desire is wholeness, freedom, and sustained strength.

DELIVERED FROM EVERY AFFLICTION!

PRAYER AND DAILY DECLARATION

HEAVENLY Father, I thank You for being my Healer and my Protector. You are not only the One who restores, You are also the One who preserves. You have delivered me from past afflictions, sustained me through weakness, and placed a boundary of mercy and protection around my life. Nothing touches me without passing through Your sovereign hand. I receive Your promise of divine health with faith and gratitude. I release every fear of sickness, every anxious thought about my body, and every lingering memory of past affliction. I will not allow past experiences to shape my expectations. My confidence is rooted in Your covenant, not in former battles. Let Your covenant of health remain active in my body, my mind, and my household. Strengthen every system, regulate every imbalance, and fortify every vulnerable place. Where there has been strain, restore strength. Where there has been weakness, establish resilience. Today, I decree and declare that the Lord takes sickness away from me. Affliction has no permanent place in my life. My body is preserved by God's power. I walk in divine health and sustained strength. What God has delivered me from will not return. I am covered by covenant. I am strengthened by grace. I am kept by the faithful hand of my God. I stand confident, whole, and preserved, not fragile, not fearful, but upheld by divine protection. My life reflects health, stability, and the sustaining power of the Lord. In Jesus mighty name, Amen

SCRIPTURE READING

REFLECTION AND ENCOURAGEMENT

This passage celebrates the beauty and discipline of intentional gratitude. It declares that thanksgiving is not merely a response; it is a good thing, a wise and life-giving practice. To begin the day acknowledging God's lovingkindness and to end the night recalling His faithfulness keeps the heart aligned with truth and the spirit attentive to God's hand at work. Psalm 92 reminds us that God's works are great and His thoughts are deep. Not everything He does is immediately understood, but everything He does is purposeful. Growth often happens beneath the surface, and God's wisdom extends beyond what the eye can see or the mind can fully grasp. Morning praise builds expectation: it sets the tone of hope and trust for the day ahead. Night praise builds reflection; it gathers the evidence of God's faithfulness through the hours past. Together, they form a life anchored in worship, where gratitude becomes a rhythm, and praise becomes a refuge. Let this passage encourage you to thank God not only for what you clearly recognize, but also for what He is quietly accomplishing behind the scenes. Even when progress feels slow, God's works remain great, and His plans remain wise.

PRAISE RELEASES JOY AND REVELATION!

PRAYER AND DAILY DECLARATION

HEAVENLY Father, I thank You for the greatness of Your works and the depth of Your wisdom. Your ways are higher than mine, and Your understanding reaches beyond what I can see or measure. Even when I cannot trace Your hand, I trust Your heart. You are faithful beyond comprehension, and Your plans for my life are purposeful, intentional, and good. Let gratitude become my posture and praise my steady response. Teach me to acknowledge You at the beginning of each day with expectation, believing that You are already at work. At the close of each night, help me to reflect with trust, recognizing Your hand in both the visible and unseen moments. When answers are delayed, and outcomes are still forming, steady my heart. Help me trust the process of Your wisdom. Remind me that You are weaving together details I cannot yet understand. Today, I decree and declare that it is good to give thanks to the Lord. Praise fills my morning and my night. God's works in my life are great. God's wisdom guides my path. My life reflects gratitude, growth, and trust. I am not confused; I am being guided. I am not stagnant; I am being shaped. I am not uncertain; I am upheld by wisdom. I rejoice in the work of Your hands and rest in the depth of Your counsel. Your greatness steadies me, and Your wisdom anchors my steps. In Jesus mighty name, Amen.

ABOUT THE
AUTHOR

FRANNY Onokha Ofunne is a faith-driven author, visionary, and passionate encourager whose heart is devoted to helping others live anchored in God's Word. Through Scripture-based reflections, prophetic declarations, and intentional prayer, she equips readers to walk confidently in their identity, purpose, and divine alignment. With a deep love for spiritual growth and personal transformation, Franny writes to strengthen faith, restore hope, and awaken boldness in every season of life. Her devotional style blends biblical truth with practical encouragement, inviting readers not only to read the Word, but to speak it, believe it, and live it. She believes that declarations shape spiritual posture and that consistent alignment with God's promises produces lasting fruit. Her work is rooted in the conviction that God's Word is living, powerful, and actively at work in the lives of those who trust Him. Through her writing, Franny's desire is simple: To see lives strengthened, minds renewed, hearts healed, and believers established in unwavering confidence in God. When she is not writing, she enjoys reading, dancing, singing, watching movies, and spending meaningful time with her family.

www.ingramcontent.com/pod-product-compliance
Lightning Source LLC
Chambersburg PA
CBHW051950150726
47999CB00004B/1329